IMAGES
of America

IOWA STATE PATROL

Iowa Safety Highway Patrol 1935

These are the "First Fifty" members of the Iowa Highway Safety Patrol, who reported for duty in July 1935. These first 50 patrolmen, three officers, and two reservists are, in alphabetical order, Claude Benedict, Benjamin Bentzinger, William Carter, Lymane Case, James Clapp, Charles Cole, Edward Conley, Warren Crane, Donald Danford, Lyle Dawson, Clarence Day, Joe Dixon, Edgar Faber, Harold Fisher, Russell Fisher, Mark Flanagan, James Gildroy, James Gilson, Jessie Goetsch, Merle Hall, John Hattery, David Herrick, Claude Hoff, Richard Hohl, H.W. Jennings, S.N. Jespersen, James Kegley, Lou Krieger, Kenneth Lochner, James Machholz, Everette Martin, Robert Martin, William Matias, Karl Meinhard, Lloyd Meyer, Harry Nestle, Oran Pape, Robert Reese, Herbert Reynolds, Kermit Rhoades, Ronald Richardson, Samuel Shaffer, Ray Shaw, Claude Shearer, John Smith, Albert Sterzing, Stuart Stringham, Theodore Taylor, Donald Thimmesch, Wayne Ulm, Henry Weber, George Weeks, Joseph West, Mike Wilson, and Carl Wiuff. (Courtesy of the Iowa State Patrol.)

ON THE COVER: This photograph shows the delivery of Iowa State Patrol motorcycles to Camp Dodge, near Des Moines, in 1935. From left to right are Indian Motocycle dealer George Clifford, patrolman Russell Fisher, assistant chief Ed Conley, an unidentified patrol clerk, patrol chief John Hattery, patrolman Everette Martin, assistant chief Harry Nestle, patrolman James Machholz, and patrolman Claude Shearer. (Courtesy of the Iowa State Patrol.)

IMAGES
of America

IOWA STATE PATROL

Scott M. Fisher
Foreword by Mike Horihan

ARCADIA
PUBLISHING

Published by Arcadia Publishing
Charleston, South Carolina

Library of Congress Control Number: 2012950251

For all general information, please contact Arcadia Publishing:
Telephone 843-853-2070
Fax 843-853-0044
E-mail sales@arcadiapublishing.com
For customer service and orders:
Toll-Free 1-888-313-2665

Visit us on the Internet at www.arcadiapublishing.com

To the memory of Ola Babcock Miller and the "First Fifty"

CONTENTS

FOREWORD

Out of a tragedy comes a champion, Ola Babcock Miller. Prior to her election as Iowa's first female secretary of state, Miller lost a young man she loved like a son in an automobile crash. It was her goal to make Iowa's roadways safe. She did so by speaking in public, writing articles, and promoting the establishment of the Iowa Safety Patrol (now the Iowa State Patrol).

One of the articles she wrote, "The Four Horsemen of the Highway," included the Road Hog, Drunken Driver, Excessive Speed, and Unsafe Cars. She proclaimed the reckless driver as "Public Enemy Number One," writing, "No murderer or bank robber has so many victims to his credit." Today, these are the same killers the Iowa State Patrol protects its citizens from.

Miller promoted the Iowa Safety Patrol by telling the officers, "Save lives first and money afterwards." Despite opposition from labor unions and political sources, Miller captured the hearts of Iowans, and the Iowa Legislature established the Iowa Highway Safety Patrol in 1935.

In 1989, Chief Blaine Goff appointed me as Iowa State Patrol curator, which is when Scott Fisher and I first crossed paths. Scott was researching material for a series of historical magazine articles about the early years of the patrol. His great-uncle had been one of the original members in 1935. Scott and I spent many hours visiting retirees in their homes, sometimes organizing group breakfasts, or attending retiree gatherings, recording memories of those early years on the Iowa Highway Patrol. In addition, along with Capt. Shane Antle, I was responsible for the establishment of the Iowa State Patrol display at the Gold Star Museum at Camp Dodge. Many of the artifacts in that collection were donated by retirees during our visits. My wife, Jeanne, was very patient during the many years before the actual museum display was created, since our home became the "archives" for old uniforms, license plates, scrapbooks, photographs, and other historical memorabilia.

Scott Fisher spent countless hours talking to original 1935 patrol academy class members, all of whom are gone now, as well as those who followed them and current members of the patrol. I am privileged to have been a member of the Iowa State Patrol for 32 years, and I am happy that Scott has helped preserve the history of the Iowa State Patrol and captured its essence.

—Michael Horihan
ISP Badge No. 342, retired

ACKNOWLEDGMENTS

It would take all the remaining pages in this book to thank each person I have had the honor and pleasure of meeting while researching the material for this book—from members of the initial 1935 class to current troopers, officers, support staff, and family members, as well as museum curators, archivists, and Iowa historians from all over the state. I would invariably omit someone if I tried. Many have passed away in the years since this project started.

So, I will thank the man with whom this project began, the retired chief of the Iowa State Patrol, Blaine Goff, who first welcomed me to the old patrol headquarters at the Des Moines Henry Wallace Office Building, and who introduced me to the men and women of his staff, all of whom were gracious and helpful, including a newly appointed patrol history curator, trooper Mike Horihan. Mike and I began a journey that combined his interest in preserving patrol history for the yet-to-be-determined display at the yet-to-be-constructed Gold Star Museum at Camp Dodge with my interest in writing about Iowa history. It was a huge challenge—often puzzling, sometimes frustrating, but always fun.

I also thank those with whom this project comes to a close: the current Iowa State Patrol chief, Patrick J. Hoye, who enthusiastically encouraged me to pursue this book, and Amy Sturm, the secretary to the chief at patrol headquarters, who tracked down and provided me with very important photographs that were critical to the story of the patrol.

Thanks also go to the family members of all who have served and currently serve on the patrol. Being part of the "family of brown shirts," I have observed, is a special bond: one that is filled with worry, but also with pride.

Finally, thank-yous go to all the men and women of the current patrol who are dedicated to continuing Mrs. Miller's vision of promoting highway safety for all Iowans, which began so many years ago. Through them, her dream lives on.

Unless otherwise noted, all images appear courtesy of the Iowa State Patrol.

INTRODUCTION

It was 1935, in the heart of America's Great Depression. Iowa's cities and rural communities were struggling. America's love affair with the automobile was in full swing, but the quality of Midwest roads lagged far behind the ever-increasing power and speed of Detroit's cars. It was also the "gangster era," when thieves, bank robbers, and hijackers discovered the ease with which they could commit their crimes and escape using automobiles. No longer were they confined to just a city or county for their crimes—the entire Midwest was theirs for the taking.

Through the determination of Iowa's first female secretary of state, a widow from Washington, Iowa, named Ola Babcock Miller, a much-debated and often-opposed bill was signed into law that created Iowa's first state law enforcement agency. More than 3,000 men applied for the new positions. About 100 were invited to Camp Dodge, near Des Moines, for the first Iowa Highway Safety Patrol training camp. After weeks of physical, psychological, and technical training, 50 men were selected.

They came from all over the state, from all walks of life, most of them without any formal law enforcement experience or even military training. All had been interviewed personally by Miller and then carefully scrutinized by the newly appointed patrol chief, John Hattery, and assistant chiefs Harry Nestle and Edward Conley, who planned, organized, and ran the paramilitary-style training camp. The recruits came from small towns, cities, and farms throughout the state. Many of them had been high school and college athletes. Some were single; many had families. They were charged with the task of making Iowa's roads and highways safer for all its citizens.

The 50 men covered each of Iowa's 99 counties, some in cars, some on motorcycles, most of the time patrolling all alone with radios that could receive but not transmit. They were paid $100 a month. That was it—no overtime, no pension, no health benefits. They even had to buy their own ammunition. But it was a steady job when so many desperately needed one. They became part of the communities to which they were assigned and spread the word about highway safety, often on their own time. "Mrs. Miller's boys" were a special group whose efforts drastically reduced highway deaths and rural crime almost immediately. They started a tradition that has been passed down to a modern Iowa State Patrol, which has undergone necessary changes through the years but is always based on what those "First Fifty" created: a trust with Iowa citizens.

Those men are all gone now. "Buck" Cole, the last retiree, passed away in 1999. My great-uncle, Russell J. Fisher, was one of those men. He seldom talked about his days on the patrol, but I heard the stories about him from his brothers and nephews, and, later, from his fellow patrolmen. I was fortunate to be able to interview some of the "First Fifty" members, as well as many who were trained by them and who, in turn, trained today's patrol members. Modesty is one of many traits they all shared, as well as a sense of pride in being part of something that grew to be one of the most respected state law enforcement organizations in the country. But to them, it was "just the job" they were given. Even into their 80s and 90s, these men, and the men and women who came after them, retained the philosophy drilled into them from the first training camp, which continues today: Courtesy-Service-Protection for those who use Iowa's roads. That kind of training never leaves a person, no matter how old he or she gets, nor does the willingness to help others in times of need.

I think this can be illustrated by relating an incident that happened to my uncle Russ many years after he had reached retirement age. One day, while working at Olson's Boat House in Cedar Falls, he was servicing the fishing boats along the Cedar River when he heard shouts for help. He looked up and saw some boys in a boat heading for the dam. Russ got into a boat and headed out onto the river to try to keep the boys' boat from spilling over the dam. He managed to get to their boat and grab hold of it, but the current was too strong and they all went over the churning waterfall of the dam. One boy drowned, but Russ and another boy survived. The ordeal took a physical toll on him from which he never fully recovered. He had acted instinctively, just as he had when lives were in the balance during his days on the patrol.

So this is their story, told as much as possible in their own words, collected during retirees' gatherings, at kitchen tables, and in living rooms, from Des Moines to Strawberry Point and from Council Bluffs to Keokuk, wherever I could find a retired patrolman and members of his family willing to share their stories. Stories were also collected from numerous ride-alongs and fly-alongs and in diners and coffee shops along Iowa's roads, where I listened to modern-day men and women troopers who graciously gave their time.

This book contains only some of the highlights, as space permits, of more than 75 years of the patrol, and of some of the events in Iowa history with which the troopers were involved, often making the difference between life and death. I encourage you to visit your local library and museum to learn more of the details about the patrol's history as it relates to your own community. Also, next time you are at your local county fair or the Iowa State Fair, visit with a trooper. You will find him or her to be genuinely interested in visiting with you and talking about the patrol and its legacy.

One

IOWA'S EARLY ROADS

"Choose your ruts carefully: you'll be in them for a long time." Those were the common words of advice for Iowa motorists brave enough to attempt cross-country driving in the early 1900s. The new horseless carriage was nothing more than a motorized buggy, but it captured the imagination of Americans from coast to coast. Between 1895 and 1904, the number of motorized vehicles on US roads skyrocketed—from just four to more than 55,000. So, in 1904, the Iowa Legislature created the first Iowa Highway Commission, with Charles F. Curtiss and Anson Marston named as the first commissioners charged with improving Iowa's roads. Thomas H. MacDonald was put in charge of "field operations"—a very appropriate title, since that is where most of his work would take place. (Courtesy of the State Historical Society of Iowa–Iowa City.)

In order to fund some of the road improvements, the office of Iowa's secretary of state issued the first motor vehicle licenses, which were small metal disks to be attached to the vehicle. Annually renewable vehicle licenses were $1, while a chauffeur's license, required for any driver who used his vehicle for hire, was $2. There was no examination.

Dragging the rural roads was accomplished by local farmers, who could bid on keeping their section of a road passable during inclement weather. It actually took several years to build up the kind of road surface that could withstand spring thaws and rains without turning into a gumbo on which nothing could drive. (Courtesy of the State Historical Society of Iowa–Iowa City.)

A Missouri farmer named D. Kurt King invented an effective road drag that used split logs set at a 45-degree angle. When pulled, they forced dirt to the center of the road, creating a "crown." The King Drag worked best after a heavy rain. It was pulled the length of the road in one direction, covering one half of the surface and then smoothing the other half on the return trip. (Courtesy of the State Historical Society of Iowa–Iowa City.)

Naturally, the state's dragging system had its flaws. There were complaints that some draggers collected money for work they did not do, and others about "traveling draggers," who moved in on others' territory. In response, road drag legislation was passed, along with highway-use taxes, which established guidelines, including stipulations that no one could drag for more than six miles and that no one could be paid more than 50¢ for each dragging job. (Courtesy of the State Historical Society of Iowa–Iowa City.)

START OF RACE.
PARKER IN F.I.A.T. RACER. — POUGHKEEPSIE N.Y.
ELY IN CURTISS AEROPLANE. — SEPT. 28, 1910.

The 1908 Great Race from New York to Paris passed through Iowa, following roughly the route of today's US Highway 30 from east to west, crossing the Mississippi River at Clinton. The route went through Clinton, DeWitt, Alamus, Stanwood, Mechanicsville, Belle Plaine, Chelsea, Tama, Toledo, LeGrand, Marshalltown, Ames, Jefferson, Carroll, Vail, Denison, Logan, and Council Bluffs. Montague Roberts, driving the lead car Thomas Flyer, remarked to Iowa reporters, "Everything is fine here except your roads. I never in my life saw such roads as these and I don't believe people in the east know what bad roads are. The mud, which they call 'gumbo,' is anywhere from two inches to two feet deep. My machine ought to be a canal boat." (Courtesy of the State Historical Society of Iowa.)

On September 29, 1905, F.A. Harriman, a 32-year-old attorney, along with a carload of friends and business associates, was driving his new Oldsmobile Open Touring Car three miles south of Hampton on what is now US Highway 65. Harriman and his passengers—A.W. Beed, G.F. Beed, H.L. Harrison, and N.A. Inglis—were on their way to Genoa in the late afternoon to check on some business establishments. They never made it.

Traveling at the unheard-of speed of 30 miles per hour (downhill), Harriman lost control of his car and struck a bridge abutment. The Oldsmobile flew about 20 feet in the air and landed on its side at the bottom of a six-foot embankment. None of his passengers was seriously hurt, but Harriman was killed instantly.

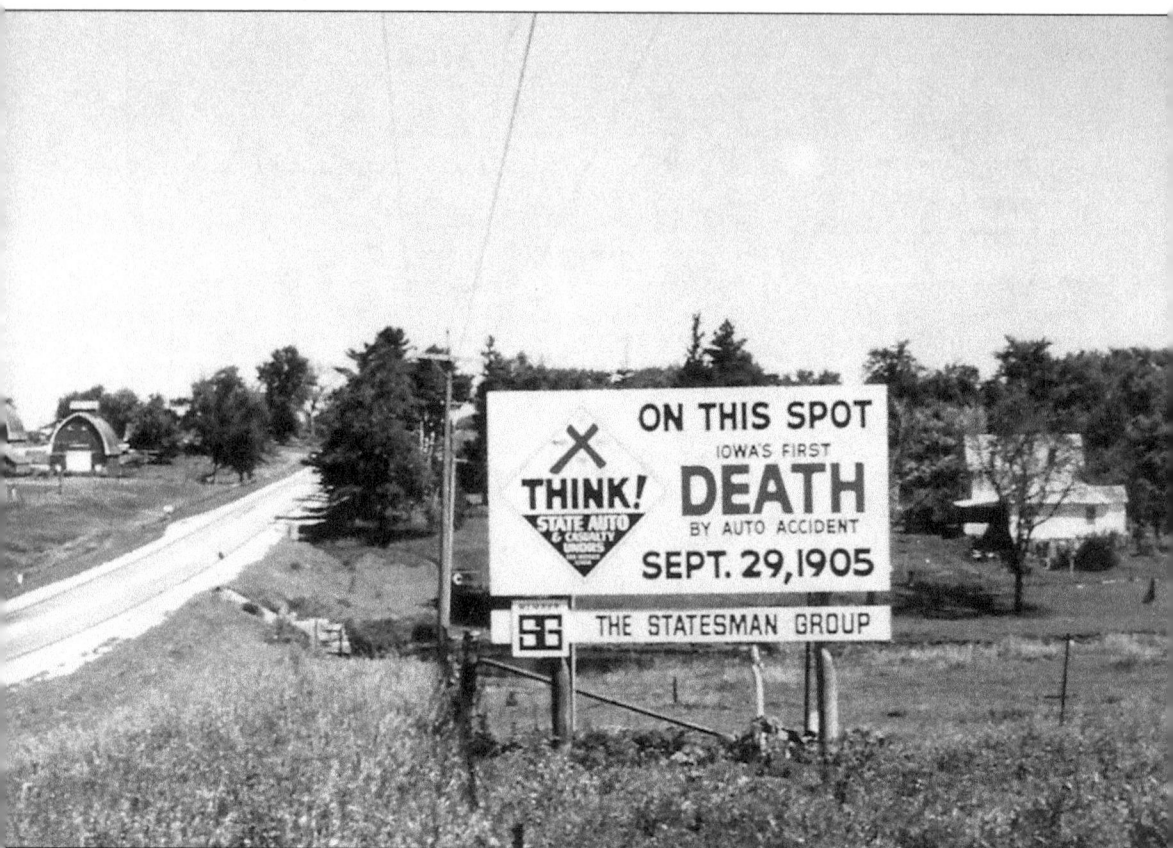

ON THIS SPOT

IOWA'S FIRST

THINK!
STATE AUTO & CASUALTY UNDERS

DEATH

BY AUTO ACCIDENT

SEPT. 29, 1905

SG   THE STATESMAN GROUP

Thus, F.A. Harriman became the first in a long line of Iowa highway motor vehicle fatalities. For many years, a sign marked the spot on US Highway 65 near Hampton. Shortly after the accident, the Iowa Legislature began debate on a number of bills that would create a highway patrol. However, it became a contentious political issue, and each bill was withdrawn almost as soon as it was introduced. Meanwhile, Iowa's population of motor vehicles grew to 20,000 by 1913, and to almost 800,000 by 1930.

Two

MRS. MILLER'S VISION

By the 1930s, Iowa's roads were improving. However, with the increase in number of motor vehicles and higher speeds came more accidents and fatalities. There was also an increase in the number of major crimes committed by outlaws using cars during the "gangster era" of the 1930s. New roads and wide distances between law enforcement agencies made Iowa a premier Midwest picking ground for bandits like John Dillinger, "Baby Face" Nelson, Alvin Karpus, and "Pretty Boy" Floyd. In a gun battle near Dexter, Iowa, Buck Barrow, the brother of Clyde Barrow of "Bonnie and Clyde" fame, was captured by Sheriff Clint Knee, who later became the chief of the Iowa Highway Patrol. Citizens clamored for more protection and better roads. Speed limits were considered for certain areas, and examinations were now required for anyone over the age of 15 who wanted to drive. A 12-question oral test was administered by the sheriff of each county and then sent to the state capitol for processing—more than 9,000 per day. Meanwhile, the deaths continued.

History was made in the 1932 elections when voters elected Iowa's first female secretary of state. Ola Babcock Miller, a native of Washington, Iowa, was the widow of well-known newspaper publisher Alex Miller. Her name had been placed on the ballot mostly as a courtesy for all the work she and her late husband had done throughout the state promoting social reform and supporting president-elect Franklin D. Roosevelt. Just before Mrs. Miller took office, a tragedy occurred that would shape her future political agenda. One of her best friends had a son, a bright young man and recent law school graduate. Just as he was to embark on his new law career, he was killed in an automobile accident. The event struck Miller as if it had been her own child. She vowed to use her new office to do everything possible to improve highway safety. It became more than an obsession; it was a relentless crusade.

Miller organized a staff of dedicated people and demanded results. She directed motor vehicle commissioner Lew Wallace and his deputy, Horace Tate, to investigate what had been successful in other states. She was not one to sit back and manage from an office. Instead, she traveled to every corner of Iowa speaking against "the enemy"—road accidents. "Good roads make for greater safety," she said, "but this is nullified by increased speed, careless driving, and very confusing traffic laws."

In addition to countless speaking engagements, Miller published essays and pamphlets to get her points across. One of her most popular described the "Four Horsemen of the Highway" which included the Road Hog, the Drunken Driver, Excessive Speed, and Unsafe Cars. She also designated the reckless driver as "Public Enemy Number One," saying, "No murderer or bank robber has so many victims to his credit."

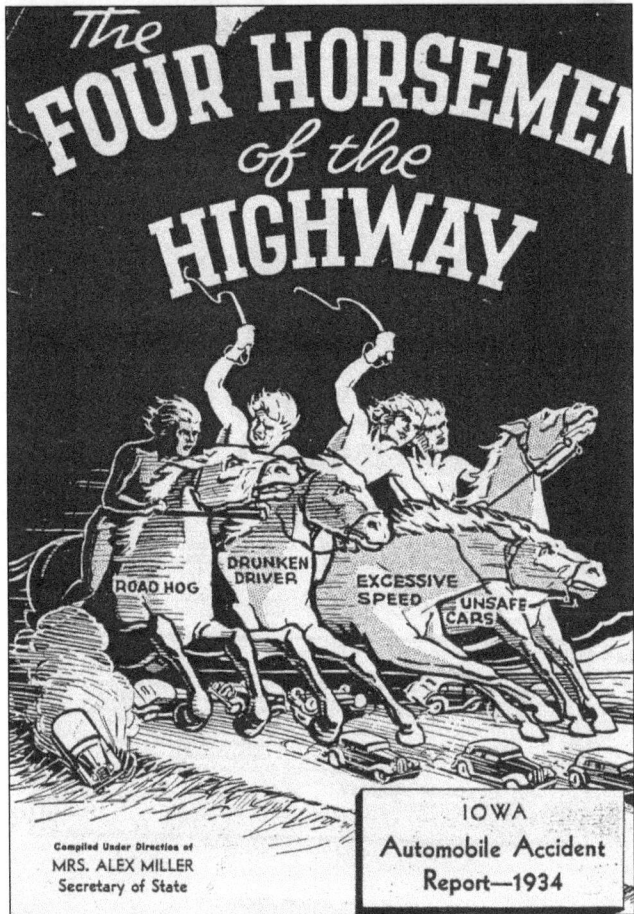

The FOUR HORSEMEN of the HIGHWAY

ROAD HOG   DRUNKEN DRIVER   EXCESSIVE SPEED   UNSAFE CARS

Compiled Under Direction of
MRS. ALEX MILLER
Secretary of State

IOWA
Automobile Accident
Report—1934

19

Part of the challenge was that Iowa's motor vehicle laws were very vague and often left up to the interpretation of individual counties. The secretary of state's office was in charge of overseeing a small group of state motor vehicle inspectors, whose main responsibility up to that point had been to make sure all motor vehicle registration paperwork was in order. They did have peace officer designation, however, and Miller decided to change their primary objective. Working with motor vehicle commissioner Lew Wallace and his deputy, Horace Tate, she devised a set of guidelines for the men to follow while patrolling Iowa's roads to enforce laws, offer assistance, and promote highway safety. Pictured here are, from left to right, (first row) Lew Wallace, Ola Babcock Miller, and Horace Tate; (second row) ? Buchanan, Harry Brown, Reuben Warner, ? Sandschulty, ? Burnett, ? Hayes, ? Russell, Clarence Shirer, and Wilbur Eicher; (third row) Harry Nestle, E.A. Conley, ? McCoy, ? Beans, ? Nugent, and ? Murray.

The men, who had been working in civilian clothes, were put in uniforms, which they had to pay for themselves, and given statewide peace officer authority and jurisdiction. Miller called them into her office and told them, "Save lives first; money after." Each man was responsible for five to six counties. She told them to keep meticulous records of their actions and progress. The uniform shoulder patch is seen here.

Their main responsibility, she told them, was to look for unsafe vehicles and unsafe drivers—to warn people about their driving habits and spread the word about the importance of highway safety. Above all, she said, "Be courteous." The men not only patrolled roads, but also spoke, as Miller herself did, at schools and with community, business, and church groups. They are seen here reporting for duty.

The program was a success. In just a few months, Iowa's traffic accidents and injuries decreased by more than 3,000. Fatalities dropped by 15 percent, while the national average increased by 17 percent. Here, inspectors cite a driver for faulty equipment. In less than a year, inspectors discovered 220 faulty brake systems, 96 defective steering systems, almost 100 improper lights, and more than 100 cars with no lights at all.

Officers inspect freight-hauling vehicles arriving at the Iowa border for faulty equipment and items such as illegal liquor and oleo, which was outlawed in the state. Behind the scenes, Miller secured approval to form an official state patrol force. "We shall always believe," she said, "that the record of this little experimental patrol was a factor in securing passage of the legislation favoring an official state patrol after it had been defeated several years in succession."

Three

First Highway Patrol Training Camp

On May 7, 1935, Gov. Clyde Herring signed the law that established a state highway safety patrol of 53 men, along with funding for a training camp. Miller and her staff had created a list of Iowa law enforcement officers that could be effective leaders for the fledgling patrol. John Hattery was the successful and popular sheriff of Story County and was selected as the first chief. Born and raised in Collins, Iowa, Hattery was paid a monthly salary of $200. Years later, after leaving the patrol to become a successful attorney, state legislator, and highway commissioner, Hattery recalled, "I had to provide directions, outline the work, and see that it was done." Hattery selected two assistant chiefs, E.A. "Ed" Conley and J.H. "Harry" Nestle, both of whom had been members of the 15-man motor vehicle inspection unit. They were each paid $165 a month. The three men began planning an intense, military-style training camp.

More than 3,000 applications were received for the 50 patrolman positions. Interviews were conducted in the basement of the state capitol building, where the patrol headquarters would be established. Here, Lew Wallace interviews candidate Russell Fisher. Applicants were required to be at least five-feet, ten-inches tall, residents of Iowa, at least 25 years of age, and "of good moral character." A college education was helpful, and former college athletes had a decided edge.

Miller conducted many of the personal interviews herself. Here, she interviews candidate James Gilson. Miller stated some of qualities she was looking for in her future patrolmen: "Intelligence—he must make decisions and handle situations that have no precedent. Courage—for moral courage to do what is right regardless of political or other pressure is a most necessary attribute. Optimism and ambition—for he must not become a drudge or get in a rut. And, above all—courtesy."

About 100 men were accepted to the first patrol training academy. They were ordered to report to Camp Dodge on Saturday, June 15, 1935. Each man was asked to bring "two suits of underwear, four pairs of socks, one rain coat, shoes for drilling, toilet articles, four face towels, two bath towels, sweater or zipper jacket, shoe polish and brush, small mirror, two sheets, two pillow slips, one bed pillow, needle and thread, laundry bag, notebook, and pencil."

Here, John Hattery (third from left) and his assistant chiefs, Ed Conley (far left) and Harry Nestle (second from left), greet the new recruits. Camp Dodge, near Des Moines, was a World War I Army base. Each man was paid $40 for the entire seven-week camp. "It was a job, and they were hard to get," recalled Karl Meinhard. Another recruit, Lymane Case, remembered, "They lined us up according to height and we were assigned to one of three barracks."

James Machholz recalled, "The entire camp was covered solid with horse weeds about ten feet tall. So we cleared our whole area—about ten acres." Buck Cole added, "They had one of the big buildings up on the hill as the headquarters and weeds, boy, plenty of 'em. So we had to clean up the whole camp. You either ran a sickle or a lawn mower—one of the two."

Classroom activities included court procedures, first aid, auto mechanics, motor vehicle law, statutory law, public relations, self-defense, and accident investigation. Buck Cole recalled, "Every Saturday morning was written exam day. At three p.m. someone at camp headquarters called out candidates' names for 'Front and Center!' Those were the men who had failed exams and who were dismissed. This went on until there were about seventy-five men left."

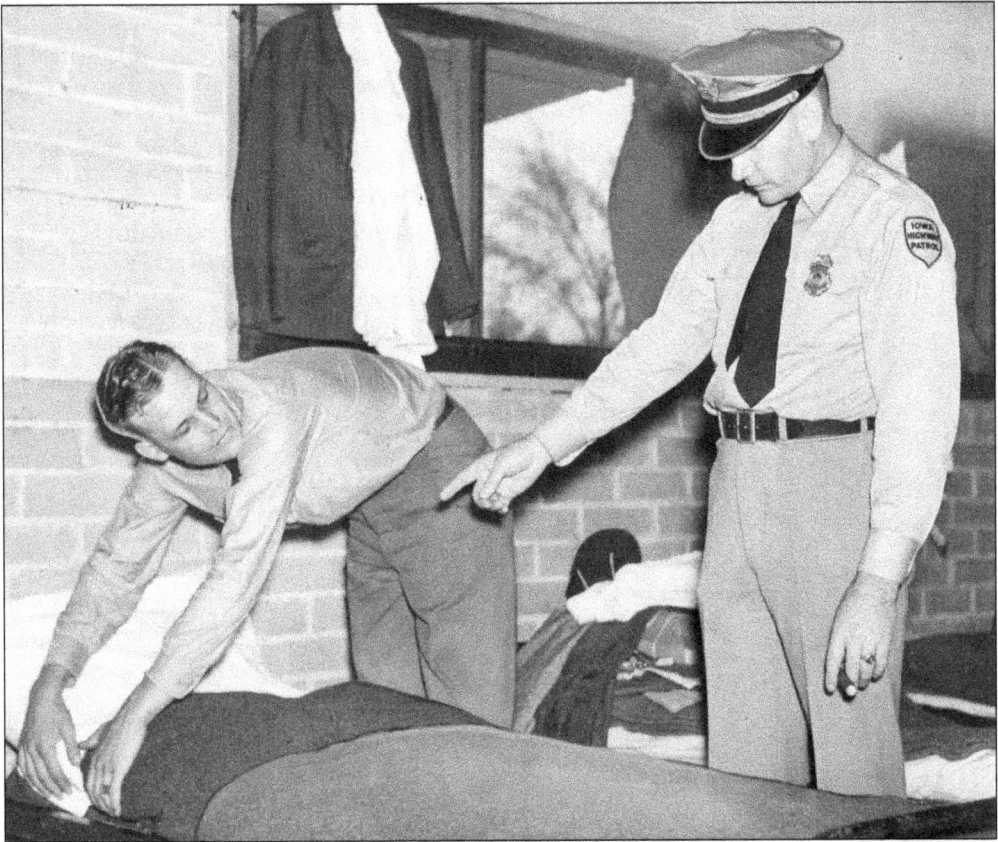

Chief Hattery inspects a recruit's bunk. The barracks, unused for years, were sorely in need of cleaning. The latrines were almost a quarter mile from the barracks. Wayne Ulm recalled: "We'd play touch football to break up the monotony. Some of us like myself, Pape, and Russ Fisher had played football at Iowa."

Chief Hattery (left) participates in jujitsu training. Several specialist instructors were brought in from other states' law enforcement agencies, such as self-defense expert Sgt. Dick Tubbs (right) of the Michigan State Police and Sgt. David Petersen of the Maryland State Police, who was the camp's chief advisor and motorcycle training specialist. Miller often visited the camp to observe the progress of the training.

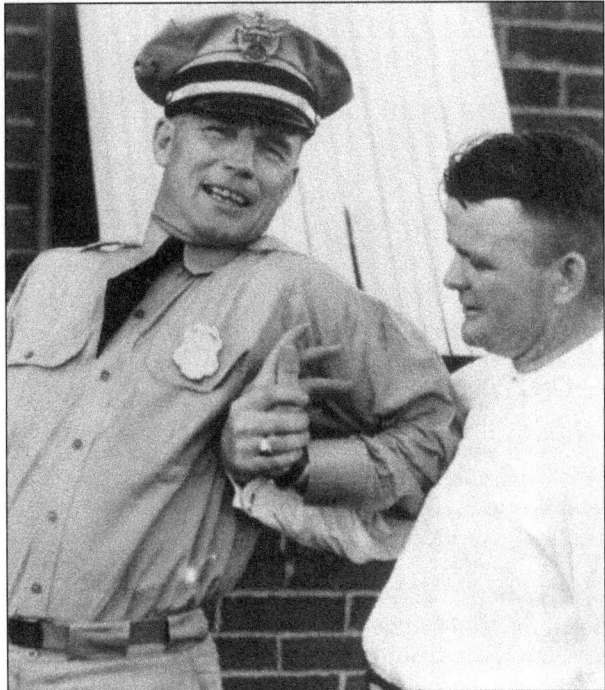

Motorcycle training was a big part of the curriculum. Lee Holt recalled, "[Sergeant Petersen] would take us out of class and give us motorcycle training. Somehow I didn't get mine [familiarization instruction] but was told to go, so I didn't want to refuse. It was muddy and raining and I drove into a rye field and all they could see of me was the rye stalks falling over as I rode through." Here, recruit Russell Fisher prepares to ride.

Lymane Case recalled, "I'll never forget Chief Hattery on a motorcycle with cigar flying out of his mouth. We got so we could ride anywhere—including ditches and corn fields." Wayne Ulm recalled, "Chief Hattery was very businesslike, very strict, but fair. Early one morning with heavy dew and wet leaves on the ground, Hattery took a ride on a motorcycle and it threw him off, but he didn't get hurt." Here, assistant chief Ed Conley takes a motorcycle ride.

By the end of July, finalists were chosen on the basis of their performance on written and oral examinations and on their physical ability. James Machholz recalled, "They had all of us in a single group and called out fifty names to form a new rank, then marched us down to the rifle range." These "First Fifty" marched in review as Miller and other dignitaries looked on.

Addressing the first graduating class, Chief Hattery said, "You are not policemen. Your efficiency will not be judged by how many arrests you make, but by the increased safety of Iowa highways." About 25 of the men not selected from that first camp were put on reserve status, many of whom joined the patrol a year later. Lee Holt was one of them, and he recalled, "They told me I didn't make it because I looked so young."

On July 28, 1935, the new Iowa Highway Safety Patrol officially began patrolling Iowa's highways. In a one-week practice patrol followed up by additional training, 38 cars and 12 motorcycles were used. For that first week, the men wore no firearms and wrote no summonses. One young patrolman spoke for his colleagues when he said, "They've done everything possible for us to make this Patrol a success. Now it's up to us and there isn't a man in the outfit who will let them down."

Four

THE "FIRST FIFTY" ON PATROL

Badge numbers from 25 to 74 were issued to the new patrolmen according to height, with the taller men getting the lower numbers. The men worked 12-hour shifts six days a week, with no weekends or holidays off, patrolling alone during the day and usually pairing up at night. Buck Cole recalled, "We got twenty-five cents for breakfast, fifty cents for lunch and seventy-five cents for our night meal. We had to pay for our gasoline, car repairs and meals out of our own pocket, then send in receipts to get paid back on the first and fifteenth of the month." Wayne Ulm recalled, "One time I needed a flashlight, and my partner, Flanagan, needed one too, so I picked them up and paid twenty cents apiece for them and turned it in on the expense account, but they turned it down. So I called [Assistant Chief] Nestle and he said to put in for an inner tube which was ninety cents and they paid that, so I guess I still owe [the State of Iowa] seventy cents."

This is the uniform hat badge. The uniform shoulder patch was also used as the patrol-car shield (see page 33). Chief Hattery and commissioner Lew Wallace created the designs. The shoulder patch was gold with black lettering that read "Iowa Highway Patrol" (today, "Iowa State Patrol"). The earlier patches resemble, and may have been meant to reflect, an ear of corn.

There is a strong resemblance of the figures on the hat badge pictured above to those on this medallion commemorating the Louisiana Purchase, which Hattery and Wallace discovered in the archives of the Iowa State Capitol. The shoulder patch's shape could also have been inspired by the shape of the medallion.

The summer uniform consisted of khaki jodhpurs and blouses, knee-high black boots, black ties, and dark brown–visored caps. Sam Browne belts were also worn at times. Badge numbers were displayed on both the breast and cap badges.

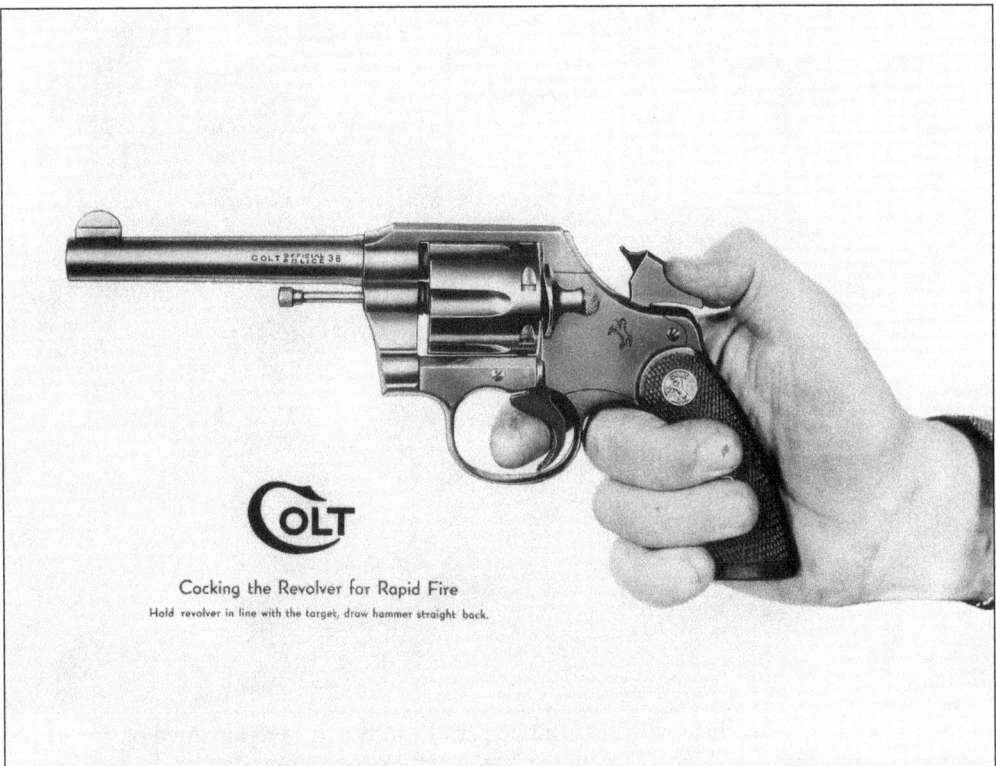

COLT

Cocking the Revolver for Rapid Fire
Hold revolver in line with the target, draw hammer straight back.

The sidearm issued to each man was a Colt .38 Special revolver with a four-inch barrel. For the first year, the weapon was holstered on the "strong side," but was later changed to a "cross-draw" location, which the patrol maintained for many years.

State Highway Patrol Chooses 19 Ford V-8's

. . . for Safety, Speed, Economy

Tomorrow, July 29, Iowa's new Highway Patrol will take to the highways to help motorists drive with care . . . to help eliminate accidents. To meet the needs for Safety, Speed and Economy, 19 Ford V-8's out of a fleet of 30 automobiles and 10 motorcycles were chosen.   Again demonstrating that the 1935 Ford V-8 is Iowa's choice.

The Ford V-8 is the Value of the year

AUTHORIZED   FORD   DEALERS   OF   IOWA

The NEW FORD V-8

Patrol cars were black and were mostly 1935 Ford V-8s (seen here), along with some Chevrolets and a few Pontiacs. Highway Patrol shields, modeled after the uniform shoulder patch, were hand-painted on each side of the car. The cars had a top speed of 65 to 70 miles per hour. Spotlights were mounted on the outside next to the windshield.

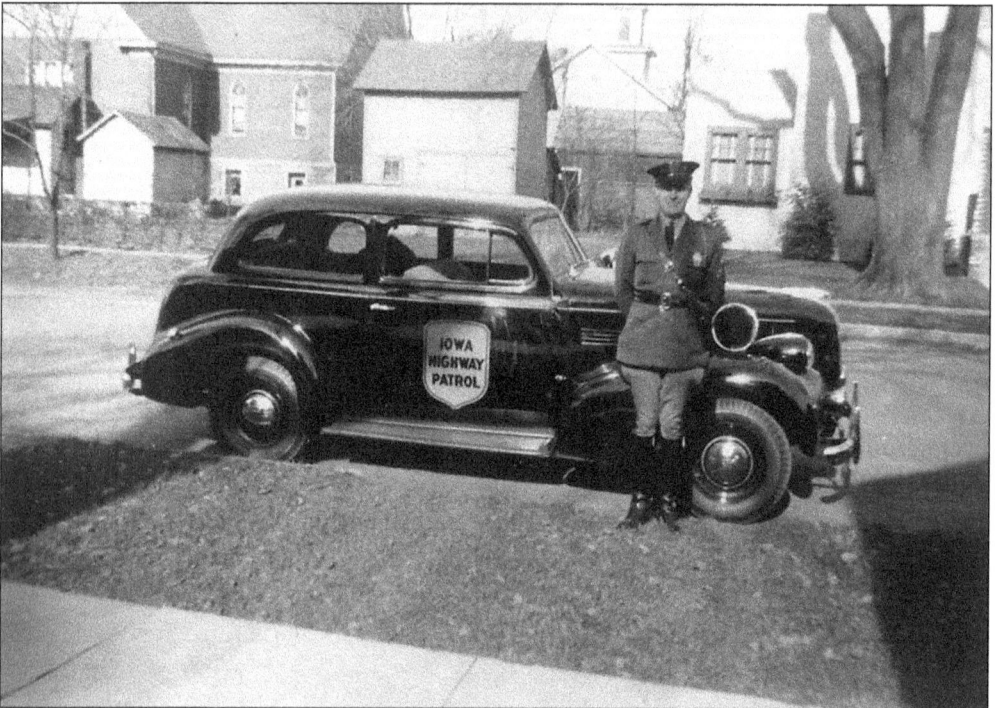

Herbert Coleman is seen here with his Pontiac patrol car. Sirens were mounted on top of the driver-side fender, and a red light was mounted on top of the passenger-side fender. This sometimes made it necessary for a patrolman to steer his car left of center when behind a moving vehicle, in order to make the red light visible in the driver's rearview mirror. Sirens were used sparingly, as they quickly overpowered the car's charging system and drained the battery.

Motorcycles were two-cylinder Indian Model 74s, assigned mostly to single men. Wayne Ulm recalled, "Those motorcycles had trouble chasing cars down gravel roads. The tires threw stones up in your face." Lymane Case added, "I was on a gravel road once and never went back—it just about shook me to pieces. I'll never forget riding in the rain on that thing—it was just like sleet hitting you in the face."

James Machholz climbs onto his motorcycle as George Clifford looks on. Machholz recalled, "We had those Bosch [radio] receivers on the handlebars. So, when you had an accident, that's where your head went. We didn't have any helmets. There was a big grasshopper plague in 1936—it was tough riding through those. After riding all summer, your face was brown/black except where your sunglasses were. You looked like an owl."

Patrolman Traverse Grimm is ready for motorcycle duty. Motorcycles were ridden until late fall, when men switched to cars until early spring. Occasionally, a motorcycle officer was forced by severe weather to seek shelter in a farmer's barn and either wait out the storm or call—if the farm had a telephone—for a patrol car to come and pick him up so he could finish his shift.

Patrol posts were set up across the state, which was organized into two districts: east and west. Assistant Chief Conley was in charge of the east district, while Assistant Chief Nestle supervised the west district. Men paid their own moving expenses to their assigned community, but, with the times being hard, Miller frequently subsidized many of the men's expenses out of her own pockets.

Here, a young patrolman visits with some rural drivers. Patrolmen were on their own when enforcing Iowa's vague traffic laws. Wayne Ulm recalled, "One time I picked up one guy who was driving all over a gravel road. I ticketed him for driving on the wrong side of the road. He took it to court and his attorney argued there was no 'wrong side'—that vehicles only needed to pull to the right when meeting oncoming traffic. He won."

Rough roads and older vehicles ensured breakdowns and "motorist assists" such as this one, with patrolman Russell Fisher helping a driver change a tire. Chief Hattery recalled, "I used to read the daily report of each patrolman and I noticed that one patrolman was claiming thirteen assists rendered on a rather sparsely traveled highway one morning. Upon questioning I found that he had stopped his motorcycle and driven an old sow and twelve piglets off the highway."

Patrolman William Matias cites the driver of a pickup that had collided with a team of horses. It was not unusual for a patrolman to complete his 12-hour shift, then return home to spend several hours doing his daily report, which was sometimes interrupted by a call to drive to the scene of a traffic accident. The men had special training in accident investigation, which county and local authorities often requested at any time of the day or night.

Following the same accident, patrolman Matias tries to render first aid for the pickup truck driver, who suddenly suffered a seizure as a result of scarlet fever. The driver later died. Since the patrol cars' radios could not transmit, only receive, the men were truly on their own. Karl Meinhard recalled, "Sometimes all you could do was wait [for professional medical help] and try to make them comfortable."

The Cedar Falls police radio station is seen here. At first, state police radio stations broadcast bulletins only three times a day, so a patrolman had to be sure his vehicle was in a good location to receive the AM signal. Later, bulletins were broadcast as soon as they were received, but only from 8:00 a.m. to 5:00 p.m. six days a week, because that was when most crimes were committed.

H.H. Joy was the chief operator for the state police radio station at the Iowa State Fairgrounds in Des Moines. Here, he adjusts the controls of a new AM transmitter in 1937—note the large vacuum tubes. It would be another 10 years before the system switched over to FM and patrolmen had the capability to both send and receive from their cars and motorcycles.

MANVILLE
MANUFACTURING CORPORATION
PONTIAC, MICH.

To protect your men throughout the year
With that balance of power that criminals fear
Means only to budget a very small sum
To purchase the new Manville Tear Gas Gun,
We hope you haven't lost a man
That could have been saved by the tear gas plan

Wishing You
A Merry Xmas and a Happy New Year

The Manville Mfg. Corp.
Pontiac, Michigan

MANUFACTURERS OF MULTIPLE
FIRING TEAR GAS EQUIPMENT

Part of John Hattery's job as patrol chief was maintaining his budget and dealing with vendors trying to sell him equipment. This cleverly rhymed Christmas greeting was sent by a hopeful vendor of tear gas guns. It was found in Hattery's scrapbook by his son Robert. (Courtesy of the Hattery family.)

Patrolmen are seen here in the first winter uniforms. Donald Thimmesch is on the far left. In the winter months, the men were issued wool, olive drab uniforms that included waistcoats over their shirts. They were also issued heavy wool overcoats. Buck Cole recalled, "That first winter was the coldest in Iowa history and some of us didn't have overcoats at first. We just pulled on sweatshirts—all we could get on and still button our shirts."

School bus inspections were part of the job each fall, along with making sure schoolkids were protected on roads during bad weather. Once, during a blizzard, patrolman Lyle Dawson found the Early, Iowa, school bus stuck in the snow. The driver had gone for help and left the bus running, and some of the children were overcome by carbon monoxide. Dawson put the children into his patrol car and drove them to a doctor. His daily report described the incident as simply a "motorist assist."

This photograph shows patrol update training at Camp Dodge. Patrolmen were often assigned to refresher training, where road patrol experiences were shared. James Machholz held the distinction of being the first officer fired upon. "I was riding a motorcycle near Hinton, Iowa, and approached this car with two men and one woman in it. I got within a hundred feet of it and one of the occupants starting shooting at me with a rifle. I fired back with my revolver and hit it, but it turned off on a side road and got away. There was no way our motorcycles could chase down a fast car."

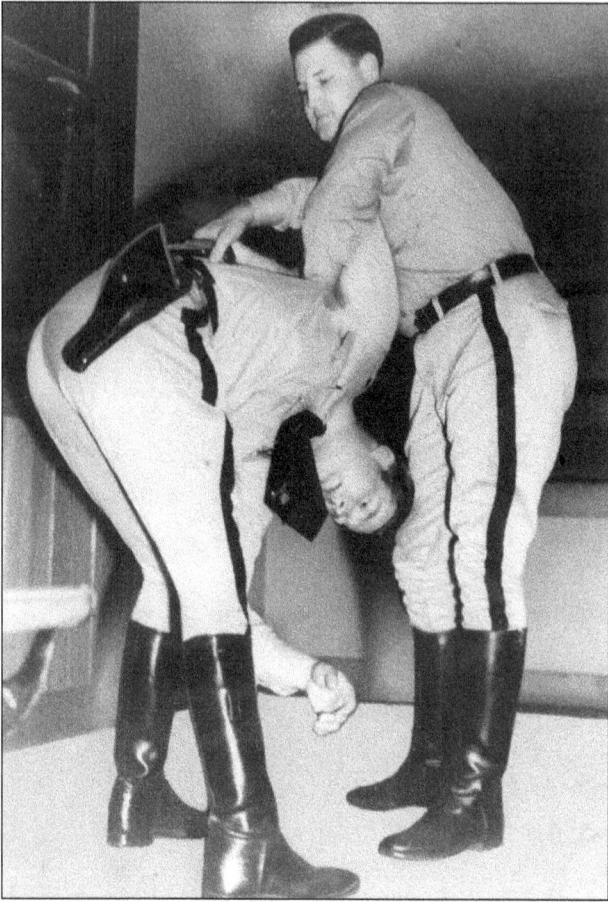

Self-defense refresher training is seen here. Chief Hattery was usually on had to supervise the refresher training sessions. The men, as well as their commanding officer, were learning on the job as unforeseen events arose. Hattery recalled, "It was not unusual for me to receive an average of three to five calls per night between midnight and morning from various patrolmen who were confronted with situations that had not been covered in the school."

Fairport Fishery and Biological Research Station is on Iowa Highway 22 (old US Highway 61) along the Mississippi River near Muscatine. The site has not changed much since April 29, 1936, when a gunfight took place that mortally wounded Oran "Nanny" Pape, the first officer of the patrol to be killed in the line of duty, and the only one to be killed by gunfire. (Photograph by the author.)

Oran "Nanny" Pape was a native of Dubuque who had been a standout football player for the Iowa Hawkeyes in the late 1920s and later played semiprofessional football in Ohio. He was selling insurance back in Iowa when the opportunity to join the patrol came his way. He was one of the "First Fifty"; his badge number was 40. Lymane Case, another First Fifty patrolman who had played center with Pape at Iowa, recalled, "Pape and I used to meet on Highway 61 [now Highway 22] every once in a while." On that fateful day in April, Pape was nearing the end of his shift and traveling northeast near the fishery. He came upon a black Chevrolet sedan that he determined was stolen. The driver was 23-year-old Roscoe Barton of Davenport, a parolee from Leavenworth and a known thief. Pape motioned for Barton to pull over. As Pape approached the stolen car, Barton pointed a .45 automatic at the officer, took his .38 service revolver, and ordered him into the passenger's front seat. Covering Pape while he drove, Barton wedged the officer's revolver between the seats.

At some point, while Barton was shifting gears on a curved hill, Pape grabbed the driver's wrist, knocking the .45 into the back seat. Barton grabbed Pape's revolver, pressed it against the officer's abdomen, and fired. The car went off the road as the two men struggled for the gun, with Barton kicking and scratching at Pape's eyes. The gun's muzzle then steadily turned toward Barton's face and went off, killing him instantly. (Photograph by the author.)

Pape was bleeding badly as he crawled out of the car and onto the road. Passing motorists stopped and transported Pape to Muscatine's Hershey Hospital, where he died that night. Pape's badge number 40 was permanently retired. He was buried in Dubuque's Linwood Cemetery. Recently, the Iowa Department of Public Service office building in Des Moines was renamed the Oran "Nanny" Pape Building. The westbound Interstate 80 bridge traversing the Cedar River at mile-marker 265 was also dedicated to Pape. (Photograph by the author.)

Five

CHALLENGES
AND CHANGES

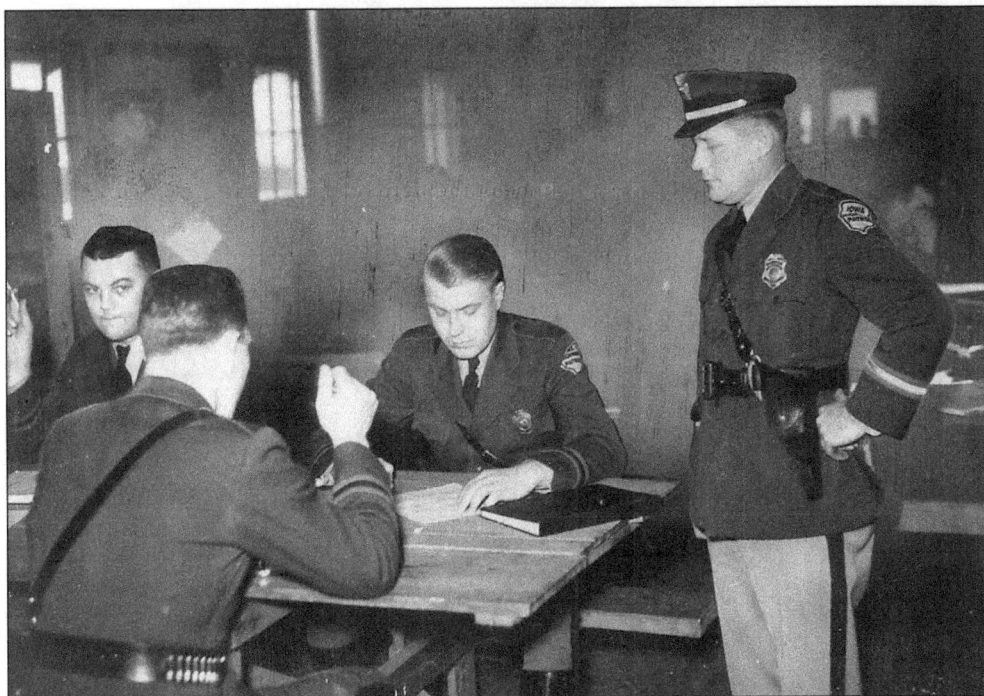

Retraining was intensified following the death of Nanny Pape. Sessions were scheduled for everyone at Fort Des Moines to explain changes in patrol guidelines and procedures. Written tests like this one, monitored by Assistant Chief Harry Nestle (far right), were administered to check officers' knowledge before heading back into the field.

A refresher course in self-defense and disarming a suspect was required for all patrolmen. Officers were now permitted to approach suspects with revolvers drawn whenever they felt it was necessary. Previously, a patrolman could not draw his weapon unless "faced with hostilities."

The men were drilled over and over, reenacting many different possible scenarios that they might face both in rural areas and on busy city streets. "Not everything they learned at the training camp prepared them for the 'real world,'" Chief Hattery explained. "We had to add new tactics and make modifications based on what the men saw out there on the road."

The patrol force was divided into two groups for the update training, with each scheduled for different times to minimize interruption of the patrolling of the highways, even though the actual number of men available for road duty was cut in half for a two-week period. Here, the officers practice on the pistol range. Patrolmen were required to pay for their own ammunition.

Another change was the patrolman's service revolver holster being switched to a "cross-draw" position, with the butt of the gun facing forward, limiting access to the weapon by an attacker. Here, Buck Cole wears the new winter uniform, which includes the cross-draw holster.

Miller had compiled statistics proving how effective the patrol was in reducing traffic fatalities. An increase in license fees to 50¢, she proposed, could fund an increase in manpower for the patrol, which could also administer written and behind-the-wheel examinations for driver's licenses. A new designation of "Drivers Examiner" would be established. This is the shoulder patch, identical in shape, size, and color to a patrolman's.

The breast and cap badges were also the same as a patrolman's. Driver's license examiners were required to participate and pass the same training as patrolmen, and could be moved to road duty at any time. A new training camp was approved, with 85 recruits. Ralph Vermillion, a member of that first class, recalled, "They pounded it into you that it was a *safety* patrol and we should do everything possible to make highways safe."

48

A woman receives her new driver's license from an unidentified drivers examiner (far left). Licenses were renewable on July 5 of each odd-numbered year. This system, with patrolmen administering behind-the-wheel examinations, continued into the 1970s.

Here, Don Thimmesch (left) works on patrol reports with the help of an unidentified post clerk. Ralph Vermillion recalled, "I was amazed at all the paperwork. The daily reports were very thorough." Assistant Chief Ed Conley called for an enforced speed limit—at the time, the only posted warnings called for a "Safe and Prudent Speed." He said, "The only way we can hope to make any appreciable decrease in accidents is to control the speed which we cannot do without a speed limit being placed on drivers." It may have been Conley speaking, but it was Miller's continued crusade.

Miller never lived to see the increases in patrol manpower or funding. In early January 1937, after a long speaking tour across Iowa, she became seriously ill with influenza and needed to be hospitalized. She insisted that nobody send flowers, but members of the patrol sent dozens of them. "That's the only time they have ever been guilty of insubordination," she said. She died on January 24, 1937. It was the second time in less than a year that patrolmen wore black armbands in memory of one of their own.

More than 1,500 people attended her funeral in Washington, Iowa, which included an honor guard of "her boys," all of whom attended.

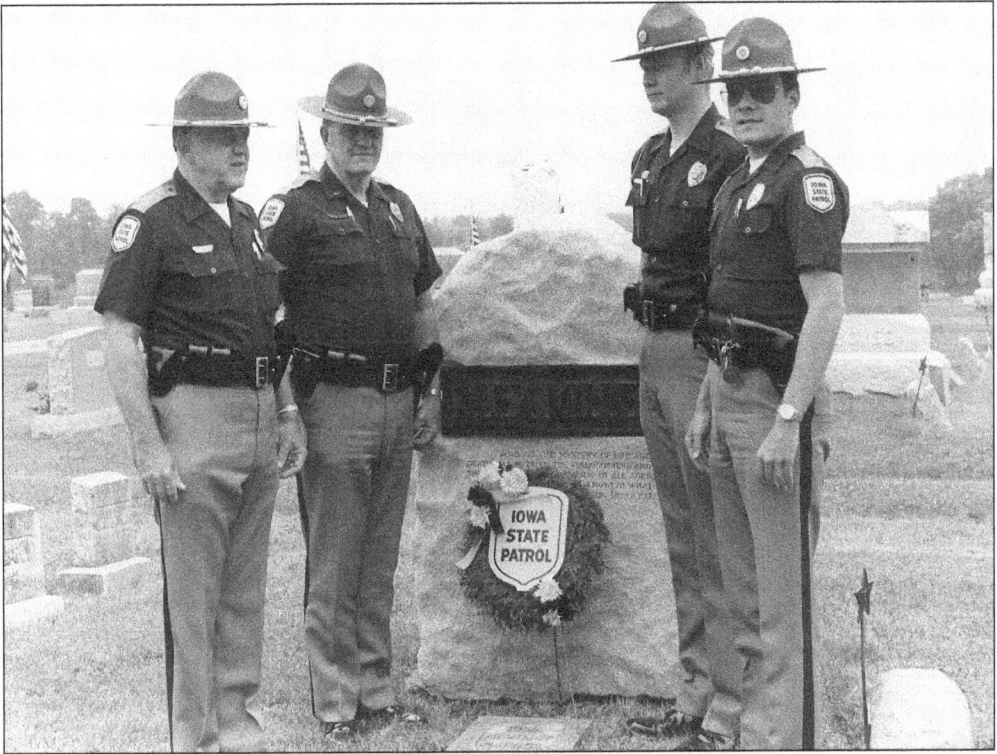

Miller was buried next to her husband in Washington, Iowa. Her gravesite is visited each year by members of the patrol in memory of the woman who tirelessly crusaded for safer Iowa roads and who is considered the "mother of the Iowa Highway Patrol." Here, from left to right, trooper Lyle Hansen, Lt. Clinton McClintock, trooper Jay Ohlensehlen, and trooper Jeff Miller place a wreath on her grave.

Officer Leonard Sims provides a welcome motorist assist to driver George Van Zandt on a cold winter day. Above all, Miller stressed the importance of courtesy on the part of patrolmen toward motorists, which included the occasional repair of a flat tire or ride to the nearest service station for gas.

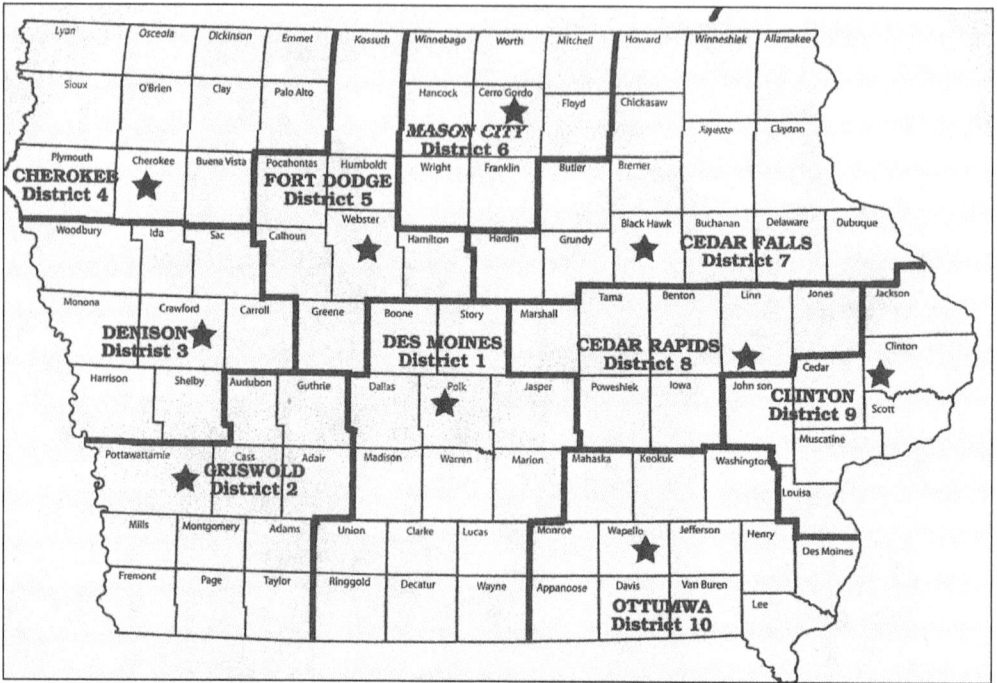

Iowa counties map with State Patrol district designations:

Lyon, Osceola, Dickinson, Emmet, Kossuth, Winnebago, Worth, Mitchell, Howard, Winneshiek, Allamakee

Sioux, O'Brien, Clay, Palo Alto, Hancock, Cerro Gordo, Floyd, Chickasaw, Fayette, Clayton

MASON CITY District 6

Plymouth, Cherokee, Buena Vista, Pocahontas, Humboldt, Wright, Franklin, Butler, Bremer

CHEROKEE District 4

FORT DODGE District 5

Webster

Woodbury, Ida, Sac, Calhoun, Hamilton, Hardin, Grundy, Black Hawk, Buchanan, Delaware, Dubuque

CEDAR FALLS District 7

Monona, Crawford, Carroll, Greene, Boone, Story, Marshall, Tama, Benton, Linn, Jones, Jackson

DENISON District 3

DES MOINES District 1

CEDAR RAPIDS District 8

Clinton

Harrison, Shelby, Audubon, Guthrie, Dallas, Polk, Jasper, Poweshiek, Iowa, Johnson, Cedar, Scott

CLINTON District 9

Muscatine

Pottawattamie, Cass, Adair, Madison, Warren, Marion, Mahaska, Keokuk, Washington

GRISWOLD District 2

Louisa

Mills, Montgomery, Adams, Union, Clarke, Lucas, Monroe, Wapello, Jefferson, Henry, Des Moines

Fremont, Page, Taylor, Ringgold, Decatur, Wayne, Appanoose, Davis, Van Buren, Lee

OTTUMWA District 10

When the approved new training camp doubled the patrol's manpower, there was a reorganization of state patrol post locations. A total of 10 districts were established, some of which also contained a number of substations, depending on district size and location. The rank of major was established for Nestle and Conley, who still supervised the western and eastern halves of the state, respectively.

Each district was supervised by a sergeant, promoted from the "First Fifty" group, who was paid $135 per month. Sgt. Russell Fisher is seen here in uniform. Sergeants spent about half their time on road patrol. Sergeant Fisher was assigned to attend Harvard University's new National Special Traffic Safety Training Program.

Sgt. Donald Thimmesch is seen here in his winter uniform. One of his duties was the implementation of speed limits, which had been established on a trial basis at three levels depending on type of road, at 25, 35, and 45 miles per hour. Safety zones of 25 miles per hour were set through all incorporated cities in the state, except where town councils set other limits.

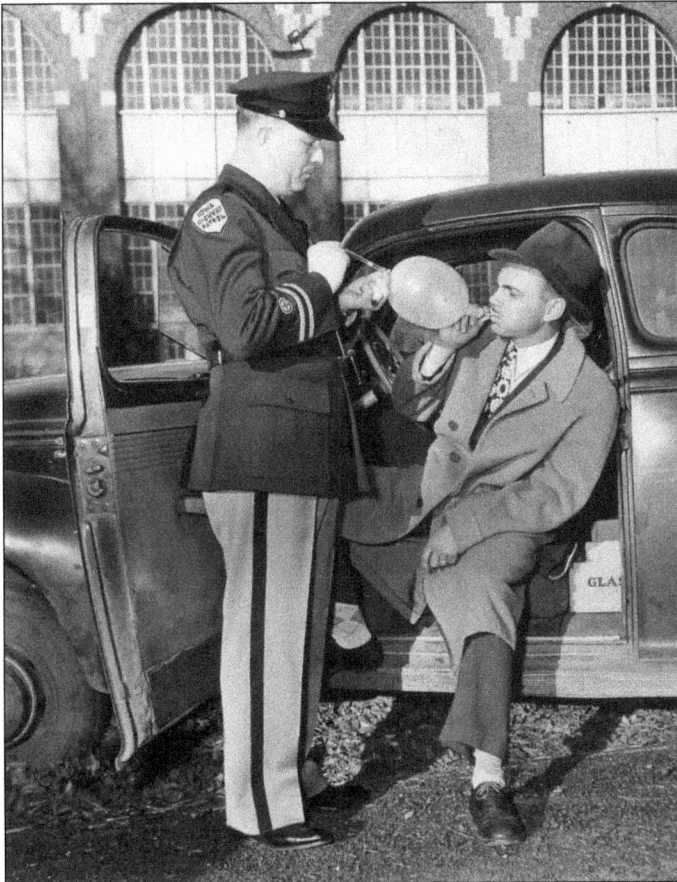

Chief Hattery encouraged patrolmen to maintain Miller's tradition of promoting highway safety in Iowa communities. Here, patrolman Ted Faber (left) demonstrates the balloon-style Breathalyzer tester at the Iowa State Fair with the help of supervisor ? Myklebust of the records division of the Iowa Department of Public Safety.

In all, 85 men were selected for the patrol's new seven-week training session at Camp Dodge. Several officials from other states were on hand to observe and participate in the camp's activities in order to create their own training programs. The format was similar to the 1935 camp. Here, the recruits are given their first instruction in the use of the Colt .38 service revolver on the Camp Dodge pistol range.

Sgt. Donald Thimmesch (center) instructs Ted Mikesch (left) and K.J. Daly in the fine points of pistol shooting. Thimmesch, in charge of one of the patrol districts, held a master rating and was a national pistol champion.

Recruits were instructed not only in proper driving procedures, but also in how to determine if a vehicle was stolen. Here, Clare Hoffman drives the patrol car while Jesse Goetsch checks the stolen car list with the radio reports. Note the "spinner knob" on the steering wheel, which helped the driver make sharp turns in the days before power steering.

New equipment was also becoming available for patrolmen to field-test cars for safe brakes. Here, two patrolman use a brake-inspection decelerometer to determine the effectiveness of the vehicle's brakes and tires. Note the unpadded steel dashboard and the non-safety, two-piece windshield.

In 1939, there was a series of changes from the top down in the Iowa Motor Vehicle Department. The Department of Public Safety was created, and John Hattery was replaced as highway patrol chief by Clint Knee, the former Dallas County sheriff who had captured Marvin "Buck" Barrow in Dexter, Iowa, in 1934. One of Knee's first actions was to establish the Patrol Special Accident Investigation Unit.

This photograph was taken near the Iowa Highway Patrol Headquarters in the Iowa State Capitol. From left to right are patrolman Mark Flanagan, patrol chief Clint Knee, patrolman Edgar Faber, and Maj. Ed Conley, who was the acting patrol chief in the weeks between the firing of Hattery and the hiring of Knee. Lew Wallace was also fired during the political restructuring.

Karl W. Fischer was named to a six-year term as the first commissioner of the new Iowa Department of Public Safety. Here, Fischer (far left) explains his plans with, from left to right, patrol chief Clint Knee, Sgt. Claude Shearer, and Sgt. Clarence Day, the latter two of whom were named patrol assistant chiefs, replacing Majors Conley and Nestle. Patrolman Clarence Shirer was named superintendent of drivers examiners.

Patrolman Ralph Vermillion recalled, "We set up weigh stations—we carried portable scales [seen here]—and helped each other stop truckers who would try to avoid scales by driving around by a side road. In Sioux City there were lots of stock trucks on Sunday afternoons heading for the stockyards. We had to watch their loads for signs of anthrax and make sure any dead animals were disposed of properly."

Commissioner Fischer promised to crack down on drunk drivers and illegal liquor transportation across Iowa. In this photograph, officers confiscate more than 1,500 bottles of illegal liquor from a 1940 Mercury that had transported the load into Iowa across the Missouri border near Mount Ayr. From left to right are the unidentified Mount Ayr city marshal, patrolman James Machholz, Ringold County sheriff Homer Todd, and patrolman Joe Dixon.

This confiscated truckload of illegal liquor is supervised by Sgt. Buck Cole (far right) in 1941 near Fairfield, Iowa. During this time, Cole suggested that the Iowa Highway Patrol adopt the motto "Courtesy-Service-Protection." The motto was officially approved by the Iowa Legislature and remains to this day.

Patrolmen were often asked to assist in the apprehension of escaped criminals. When Gordon Thompson broke out of the state prison camp at Mount Pleasant, patrolmen Nelson King and Buck Cole helped form a posse that captured Thompson near Casey, Iowa. Here, Thompson is in handcuffs as Cole (left) and King stand behind the fugitive. In the first row, from left to right, are an unidentified deputy, special deputy C.A. Bailey, Adair County sheriff E.E. Kunkle, Thompson, and Deputy Sheriff A.H. Butler.

With America's entry into World War II, the patrol's responsibilities increased. One aspect was the escort of military convoys carrying war materials, some of which were top secret, across the state. Buck Cole recalled, "We'd get a call a couple times a week that a military convoy was coming through westbound at either Burlington or Davenport. The trucks were so wide that oncoming traffic had to pull off the road onto the shoulder to pass by."

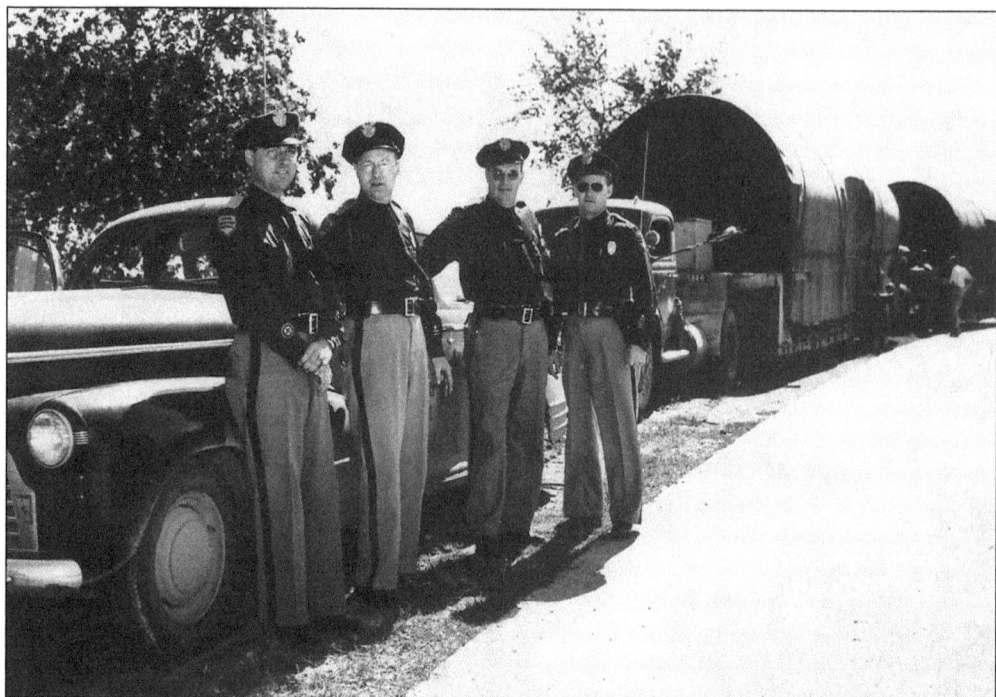

Patrolmen were exempt from military service due to the importance of their jobs, but about 60 men left the patrol to join the military, which left a depleted corps to handle the additional war-related tasks. Here, an unidentified group of patrolmen waits to escort a military convoy. Buck Cole recalled, "We were only supposed to know that they were trucks, but we knew they were hauling mostly airplane parts to Omaha for special installations for radar and electronics."

Here, the convoy and escorts organize in downtown Burlington. Bridges had to be inspected before each trip. Karl Meinhard recalled, "I was notified that the bridge between Dubuque and East Dubuque [Illinois] was to be sabotaged, and I was assigned to watch the Iowa side. I spent between fourteen and sixteen hours watching that bridge. They forgot to relieve me, or else he just never showed up. In any case, nothing happened."

60

Patrolman (and later major) John Mahnke, seen here, recalled, "We delivered sugar and gas rationing books and helped out with scrap iron drives and, of course, supervised black outs." Mahnke later enlisted in the Army. Patrolman Al Sparby recalled, "Our winter uniforms were not the best for cold weather. The winter overcoat was a navy pea coat with a small collar and our caps gave no protection to the ears. I froze both ears badly while working an accident during a blizzard."

With the end of the war, many of the men who had served in the military—like John Mahnke, third from left in the first row—returned to find their old patrol jobs waiting for them. On Wednesday evening, November 28, 1945, Mahnke was on patrol in Denison when he observed a possible stolen Hudson sedan parked on a downtown street. Before he could draw his service revolver, one of the men pointed a gun at him and ordered him back into his patrol car. (Courtesy of John Mahnke.)

The men, followed by a woman driving their car, drove Mahnke's car to a rural area, abandoned it, and forced Mahnke into their car. "They kicked my car radio to pieces," Mahnke recalled. For several hours, they drove the back roads, trying to decide what to do with the officer. "They told me, 'We had to take you. We just couldn't afford another pinch,'" Mahnke recalled. They drove to an abandoned schoolhouse near Hartley, Iowa, seen here. "They told me, 'Don't worry, John, we aren't going to bump you off.'" (Courtesy of John Mahnke.)

Using Mahnke's own handcuffs, they secured him to the grate of the school's stove, seen here. Mahnke recalled, "They threw a mattress on the floor with a blanket for me. Then they left. I was worried about freezing to death." Mahnke found an iron bar and started hitting the shaker of the furnace. "I knew nobody was going to come along," he said. "After about six hours, the cast iron structure broke." Stiff and sore, he walked to the nearest farmhouse, but they had no telephone. "They drove me to another farmhouse, where I telephoned my wife, then the Denison police." (Courtesy of John Mahnke.)

Mahnke recalled, "I was sitting there eating, with the handcuffs dangling from my wrist, when a patrol car came buzzing into the yard." It was patrolmen George Dunn and Melvin Hove who showed up as Mahnke was eating the breakfast the farm couple had prepared for him. "I just held up my hand and kept eating while he unlocked the cuffs." Here, Melvin Hove examines Mahnke's handcuffs. (Courtesy of John Mahnke.)

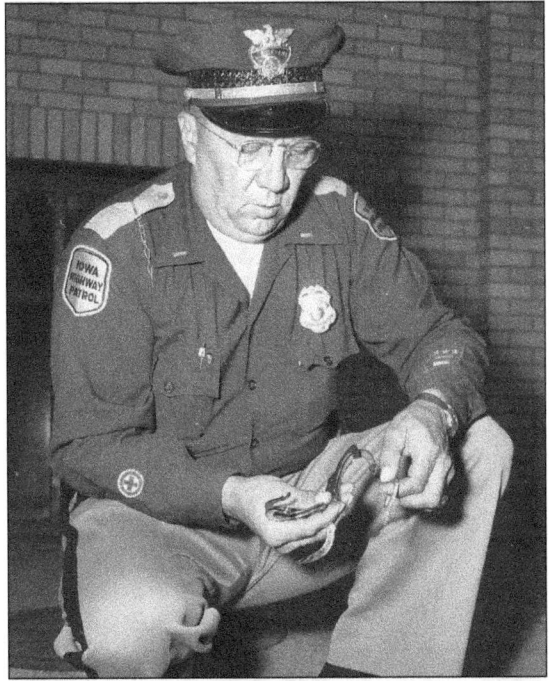

Patrolmen had been searching for Mahnke all night after discovering his abandoned car. Patrolman Lee Holt, a member of the search team, recalled, "We were up all night searching and, at one point, it turned out, within a mile of that schoolhouse." The Hudson was found in a Minnesota cornfield. This photograph shows the recovered car with two unidentified FBI agents. Three months later, a safecracking ring of five men and two women was uncovered in Chicago. Three of those members eventually admitted to kidnapping Mahnke. (Courtesy of John Mahnke.)

In March 1946, following the death of Clint Knee, S.N. Jespersen became the third chief of the Iowa Highway Patrol. Jespersen was very familiar with the issues and responsibilities regarding the patrol, as he was one of the "First Fifty" patrolmen in 1935.

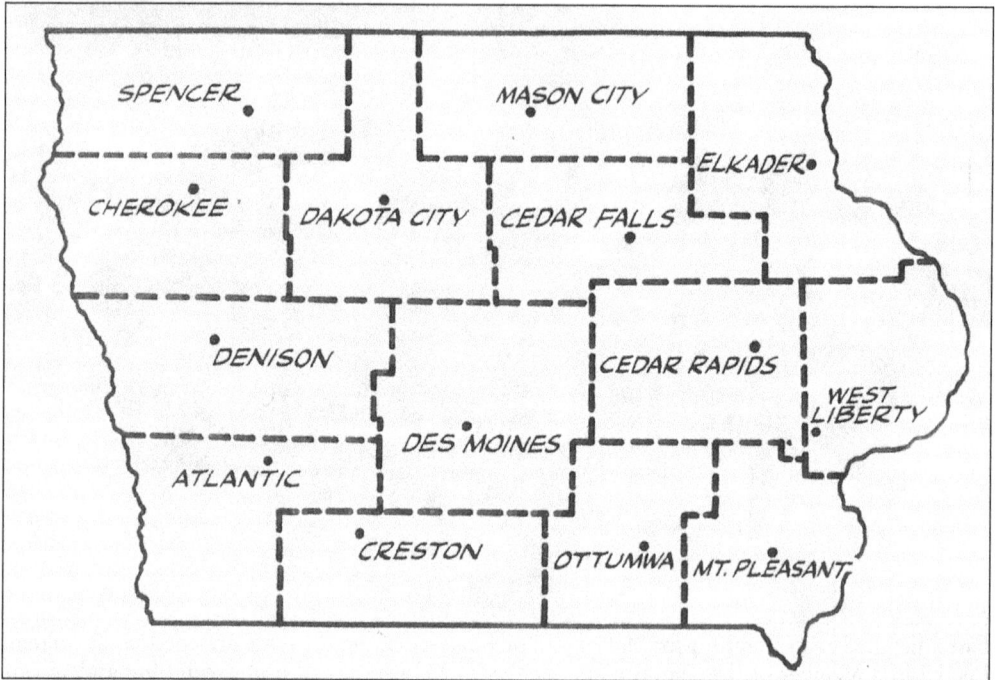

Once again, the patrol districts were realigned, and four new districts were added—in Creston, Mount Pleasant, Elkader, and Spencer. The 14 total districts were divided into four areas, each supervised by a lieutenant: Area A (southwest), Lt. David Herrick; Area B (northwest), Lt. Wilbur Eicher; Area C (northeast), Lt. Claude Shearer; Area D (southeast), Lt. Clarence Day.

64

More than 750 men applied for the first postwar patrol training camp at Camp Dodge. All 36 men who were accepted for training were veterans of World War II. James Machholz, seen here addressing the recruits in formation, was in charge of the camp. He had been one of the "First Fifty" of the 1935 camp. He recalled, "They were in better shape than I was. They were a tough, experienced group."

Harry Lown was a member of the class of the first postwar camp. Like many of his classmates, he had seen combat—more than 600 days of it in Europe. He recalled, "Claude Shearer tried to give us close order drill, but he was from World War I. We all had just come out of the service, so he got someone else to do it." The men are seen here marching to class at Camp Dodge.

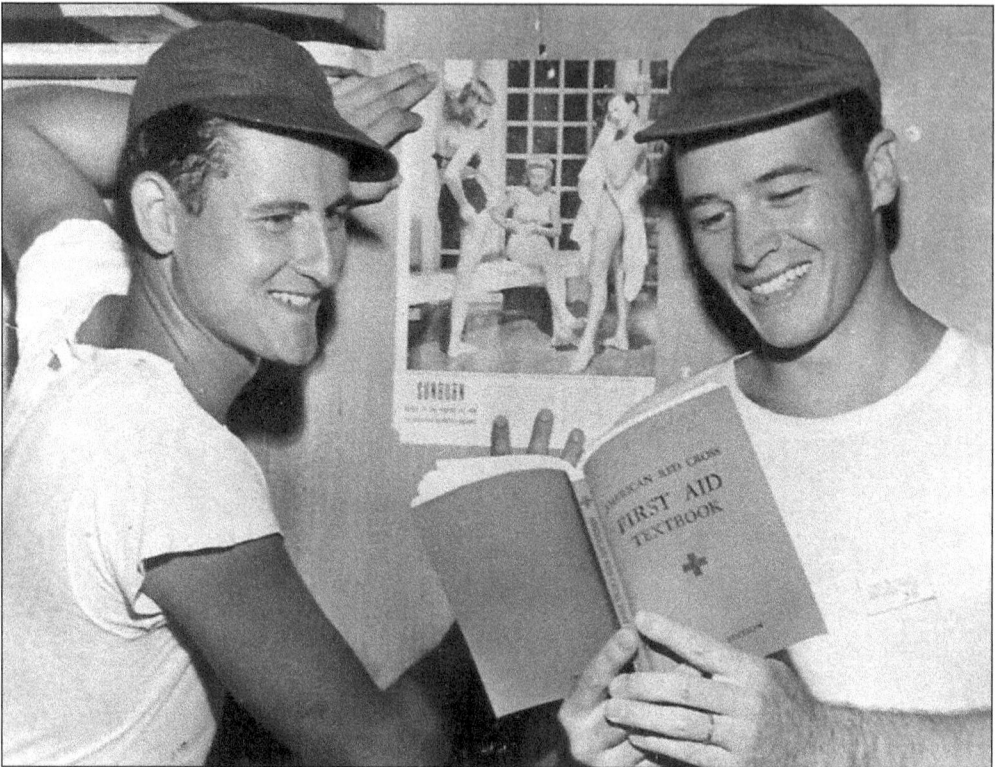

Recruits Gerald Fisk (left) and Glenn McDole of the postwar camp study first aid in their barracks at Camp Dodge. They claimed that the pinup photographs (background) were helpful in the study of sunburns for their first aid training. McDole was a survivor of the Bataan Death March in the Pacific during World War II.

Lt. Claude Shearer, kneeling on the left, supervises pistol training for the patrol recruits on the Camp Dodge firing range. Charles B. Bendlage Jr. is third from the right on the firing line. (Courtesy of Charles B. Bendlage Jr.)

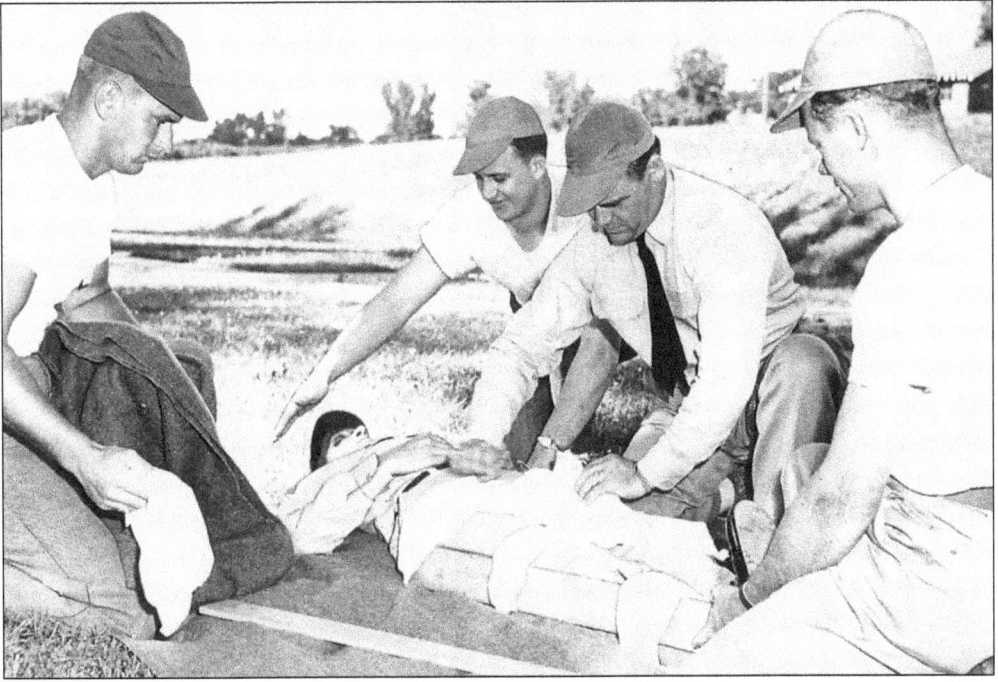

A group of recruits participates in a mock accident that requires treating an injured crash victim. From left to right are Harold DeGear, of Bellevue; the "patient," Francis MacDuffee, of Bloomfield; Wayne Soule, of Sioux City; instructor/patrolman Joe Dixon, of Humboldt; and George Ibeling, of Ackley.

Instructor Joe Dixon (standing, right) demonstrates how to apply an arm sling to a classroom of recruits during first aid training. Ralph Akers is the recruit/patient. Most of the graduates were assigned to road patrol immediately, while others were assigned to drivers examiner duties.

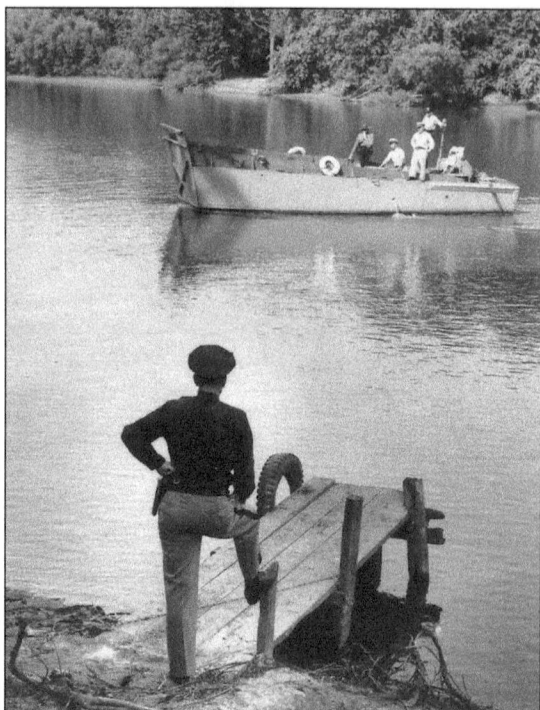

An unidentified patrolman is seen here on "dock duty." Patrolmen also helped enforce water safety regulations, as well as aiding other agencies whenever vehicle accidents involved a car entering a lake or river. Their specialized training in accident investigation was often requested when deaths resulted in rural areas. One such tragedy occurred in July 1948 near Union Mills, when six young girls died.

Helen Van Kampen had driven her brother Donald up a road near their farm to drive a tractor home. On the way back, the 16-year-old Helen, accompanied by her five-year-old sister Iva Mae, came upon the McMahon sisters, Geraldine, 15, Rowena, 14, Ila, 12, and their cousin Mona McMahon, 15, walking along the road. Van Kampen stopped to give the girls a ride on the road where it overlooked a pond. As she drove away, the car's wheel sank into a hole where the road had eroded away. The car went over the embankment and overturned, trapping the girls inside. Only Iva Mae escaped by squeezing through an open window.

Charles Nord, the director of communications for the Iowa Police Radio Network inspects the new 3,000-watt FM transmitter at the Iowa State Fairgrounds camping area, with district stations at Cedar Falls, Storm Lake, Atlantic, Fairfield, and Maquoketa. This improvement allowed patrolmen to both receive and transmit from their car radios.

Patrolman Robert Glenn poses with his 1948 Chevrolet patrol car near Lucas, Iowa. Note the front antenna, which allowed him to receive calls on his AM receiver, and the rear FM antenna for the FM transmitter. In order to pay for the new communications system, driver's licenses increased from 50¢ to $1.50, and instructional permits went from being free to costing $1.50. Only chauffeur's licenses remained unchanged, at $2.

Presidential visits to Iowa always involved increased security. The patrol provided special details of officers to escort such dignitaries. Here, Pres. Harry S. Truman (center) is flanked from left to right by patrolmen Wilton Lewis, Jim Bonstetter, Ralph Blankenbaker, and future patrol chief Edward Dickinson.

In 1949, the Iowa Legislature finally approved a pension and disability program for the officers serving in the Iowa Department of Public Safety. The bill provided a service retirement allowance, along with a disability and accidental death benefit, which was exempt from any state tax. Patrolman Harold E. Klinkefus, badge number 119, was the first member of the patrol whose family received the benefits of that program.

Harold "Klink" Klinkefus joined the patrol during World War II and was stationed in district three. On May 18, 1949, he was heading westbound on Highway 34 four miles east of Red Oak. An eastbound car was turning off the highway onto a side road, and a fully loaded semitrailer had to slow down in a hurry to avoid rear-ending the turning car in front of it. The rig jackknifed and went out of control, crashing into the side and top of Klinkefus's car, seen here. Klink was thrown clear, but landed on a fence and died within minutes.

Patrolman Klinkefus was the first officer to die while on duty since Nanny Pape's death 14 years earlier. He left a wife and two young sons. His badge number 119 was permanently retired, and a bridge on Highway 34 near the Nishnabotna River has been dedicated in his name.

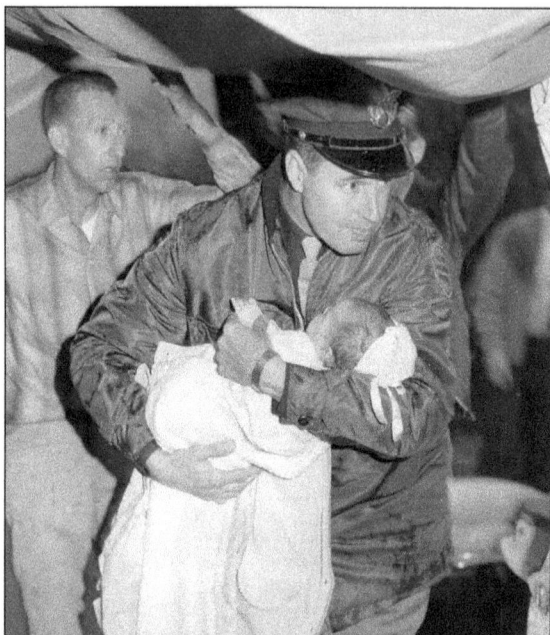

Patrolman Art Bates is seen here rescuing a baby. Preventing traffic deaths was only part of a patrolman's duties. One night, Sgt. Ted Faber and patrolman Bob Fulkerson responded to a call from the Linthicum family in Greenfield. Their five-day-old daughter Judy Anne had developed critical breathing problems and needed to make it to the Des Moines hospital, 60 miles away. With two borrowed oxygen tanks, the family got into their car ready to follow their patrol escort.

With sirens screaming and lights flashing, Faber (seen here in a local advertisement) and Fulkerson cleared the road ahead of any traffic that might slow the family's progress to the hospital, sometimes reaching 90 miles per hour. The oxygen supply was almost empty when they screeched to a stop in front of the hospital. The two officers, one carrying each end of the baby's basket, rushed her inside, where she received lifesaving treatment. Upon leaving the hospital, the patrol car's battery was dead from the extended use of lights and siren, so the officers had to push the car to get it started.

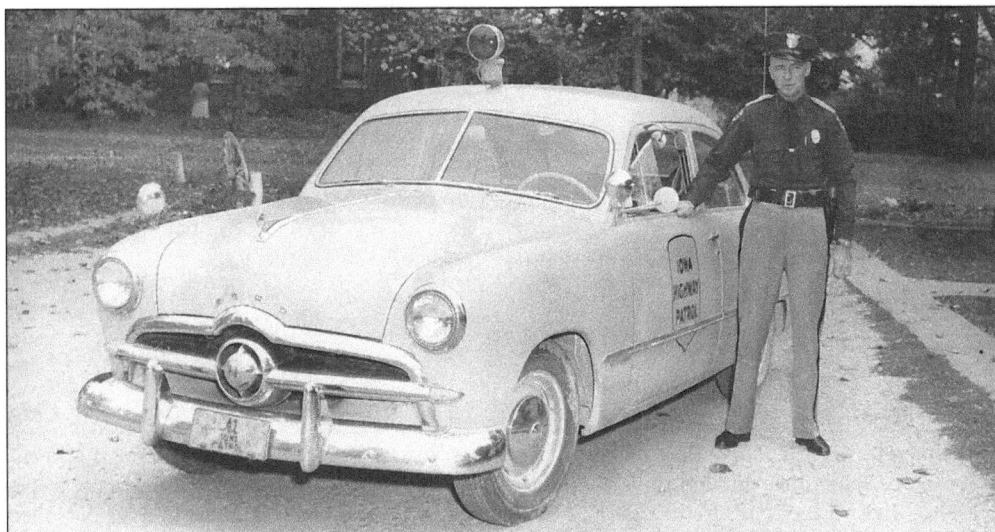

Patrolman Charles Bendlage Jr., seen here with his 1949 Ford patrol car, was a member of the postwar patrol training camp. On February 2, 1952, he was on road patrol near Bloomfield when he spotted a car that matched the description of a stolen vehicle. "I wasn't sure if it was actually the stolen car," Bendlage recalled. "But when I pulled him over and he approached my car, he stuck a snub-nosed .38 in my face and said, 'Stick 'em up! Give me your gun!' I tossed it out the window and into the mud. Just then, a farm truck drove by and I yelled at the driver to call the sheriff."

The man got into Bendlage's patrol car, seen here. "He sat with his back to the passenger's side door and kept that snub-nose aimed right at my stomach," Bendlage recalled. At the intersection of Iowa Highway 2 and US Highway 63, the man ordered Bendlage to get out, then took his patrol car, heading south toward the Missouri border. He was eventually apprehended by the Missouri State Highway Patrol. "The whole incident probably only lasted 10 or 15 minutes," Bendlage recalled. He eventually left the patrol to become a US marshal. Later, his son Chuck also joined the Iowa Highway Patrol.

Patrolmen pose with a new fleet of Ford patrol cars. Just the presence of a patrolman and his vehicle was sometimes enough to slow people down. Harry Lown recalled, "I'd often try to get out and drive all the roads in my district in one day, but I could never do it. When we patrolled at night on weekends, we'd drive through parking lots where dances were, and would walk in just to be seen and hopefully prevent people from drinking and driving."

An unidentified man helps patrolmen Peter Tometich (center) and Jack Beaman (far right, with shotgun) take custody of robbery evidence. All patrolmen were issued shotguns, though some were in used condition. Harry Lown recalled. "Mine was a sawed-off Winchester Model 12 and had a bayonet fixture on it."

74

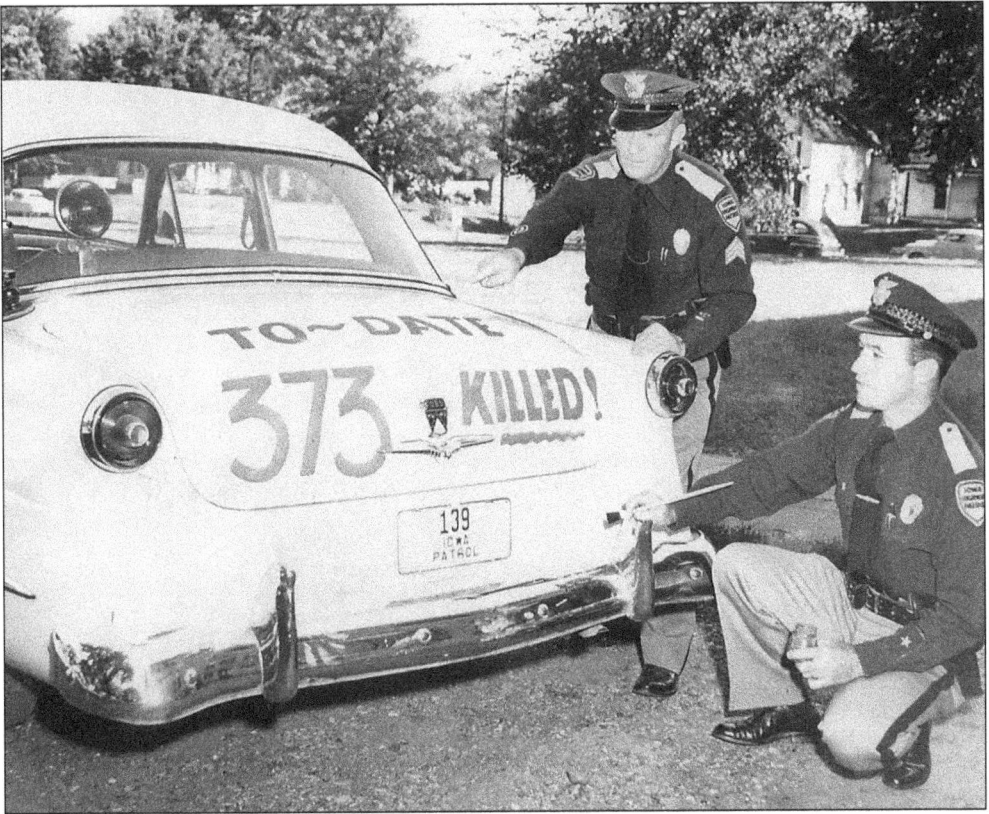

As the Labor Day weekend approached in 1953, an idea was put into place by some officers: they wanted to paint the number of people killed on Iowa roads so far that year onto the trunk lids of their patrol cars. Here, Sgt. Ted Faber (left) supervises patrolman Glenn McDole as he finishes painting the sign on his car.

The idea of painting the number of people killed in road accidents on the back of patrol cars caught the public's attention and seemed to be effective in slowing people down. So, on September 24, the patrol adopted a statewide initiative. Each morning, every patrolman checked the total killed since the day before and painted the correct number with watercolor paint on the trunk of his car. Here, some unidentified officers pose with their painted cars before heading out on patrol.

The members of the "First Fifty" were now taking on more leadership roles in the patrol. Here, from left to right, James Machholz, David Herrick, and Joe Dixon, all of them from the class of 1935, meet to plan the upcoming training for new recruits at Camp Dodge as well as refresher training sessions for experienced patrolmen at Fort Des Moines.

After seven years of duty, S.N. Jespersen resigned as patrol chief but remained with the patrol as captain in charge of the Des Moines headquarters. The new patrol chief was David Herrick, who, like Jespersen, was a member of the "First Fifty."

On a visit to Iowa, Pres. Dwight D. Eisenhower is introduced to his patrol escort team by chief David Herrick.

The patrol was often asked to relay medicine, and later, human tissue transplant materials, to hospitals and clinics throughout the state. Here, patrolmen Harold Lorenz (far left) and Bill Star deliver the first polio vaccine to an unidentified physician.

On the night of February 19, 1954, patrolman Harold DeGear, a Marine combat veteran of both World War II and the Korean War, was standing behind a violator's car writing a ticket. A vehicle that was passing a truck struck the rear of the car, crushing DeGear. He was rushed by ambulance to the hospital, where he died the next day. His badge number 60 was permanently retired, and a bridge on Interstate 80 traversing the Iowa River was dedicated in his name.

Patrolmen Howard Hays (left) and Robert Glenn perform an accident investigation near Chariton. A few months earlier, Glenn had been called to the scene of a mine explosion near Lovilia, in southern Iowa. "One man was already dead and another was seriously injured," Glenn recalled. "A doctor worked to save him while I gave him artificial respiration, but after forty-five minutes, the doctor pronounced him dead. I left, but got called back later to help the federal mine inspectors rescue some miners who had gone back in. Three of them died of gas poisoning." Glenn had also performed four motorist assists that day.

Patrolman Melvin Hove assists an unidentified motorist who had run out of gas. Hove recalled, "I arrested a 17-year-old boy for running a stop sign north of Ames. He nearly ran into my car. I told him that if he continued to drive like that he'd kill somebody or get killed himself. He just shrugged off the warning. Two weeks later he ran into a car and an old couple died. The youngster wasn't hurt—not physically. But for the rest of his life he'll remember that accident and sometimes he won't sleep so well."

Accident reports and other daily paperwork were still part of the job. Here, patrolmen Paul Mizer (left) and Georger Ponsford work on their report forms. Members of the patrol who were responsible for driver's licensing faced a monumental task. Records revealed that as many women as men were now taking the driver's license exam. The number of applicants rose to as many as 50 per day during summer months.

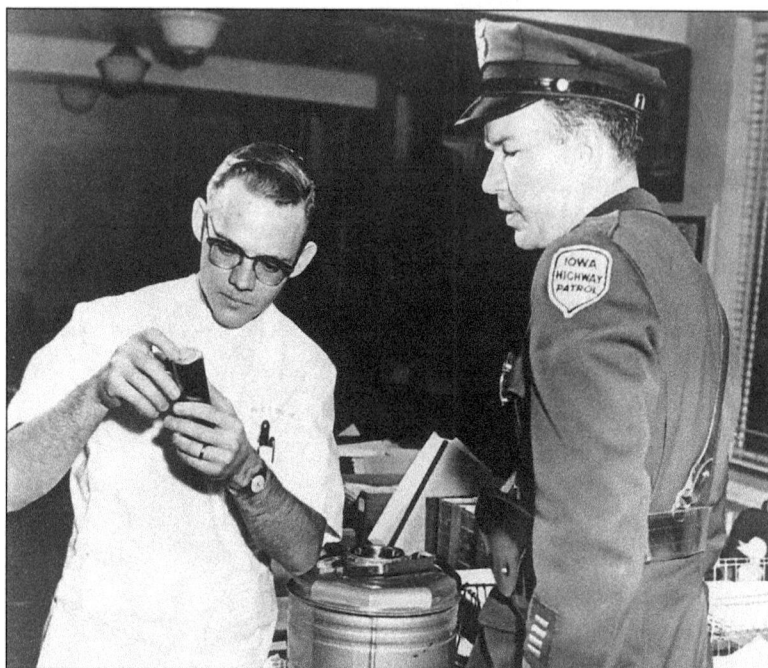

On December 11, 1955, Lt. Richard Reddick (right), of the Davenport post, made a special relay to Dr. Charles Morledge (left) of the University of Iowa Hospital in Iowa City. Lieutenant Reddick was delivering the first eye specimen for transplant. It was the first of many such tissue relays performed by the patrol.

This safety inspection check was north of Des Moines. The patrol set up many such stops across the state to locate vehicles with faulty equipment and remind drivers about highway safety. In this photograph, patrolman Jack Gorman (left) issues a faulty equipment ticket for not having reflectors to the driver of the pickup truck as Sgt. Marvin VanderLinden talks with a driver.

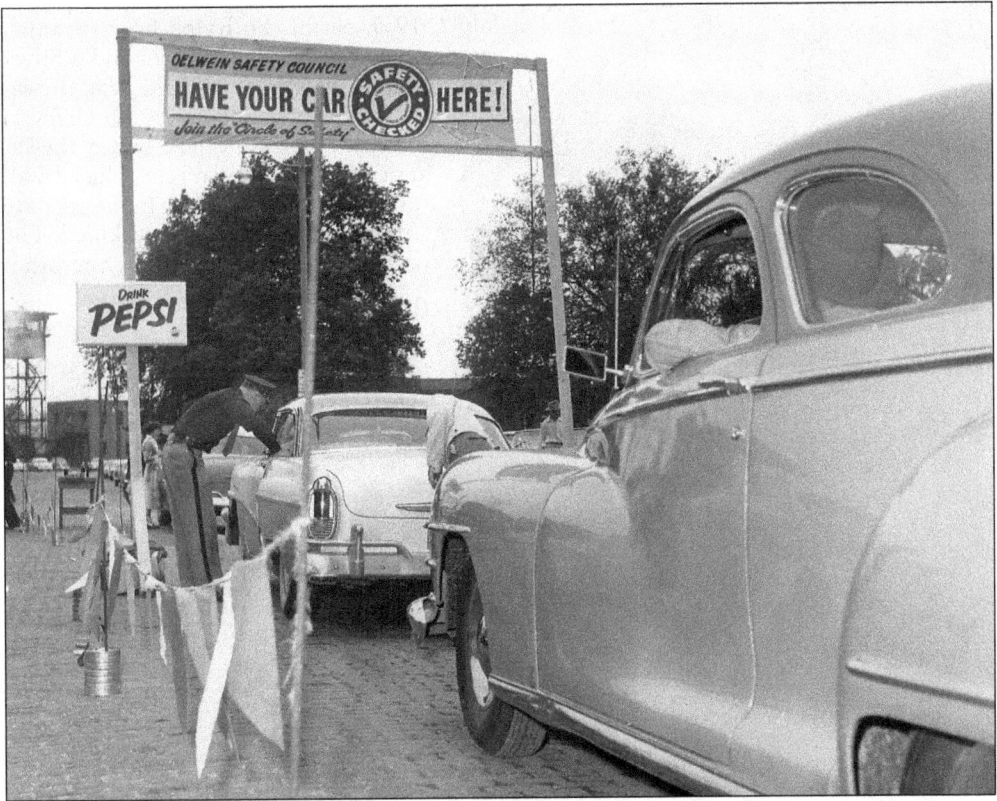

Some local organizations promoted safety checks in their own communities, such as this one by the Oelwein Safety Council. Patrolmen like Melvin Hove, seen here, were happy to oblige. Lt. Harry Brown, the assistant chief examiner for the patrol, observed, "During the first three years of driving, Iowa women show marked improvement and ability, whereas men during that same period tend to decline in ability."

While safety inspections like this one helped deter drivers from operating unsafe vehicles, the Iowa Legislature was debating whether statewide posted speed limits should be established. As a preliminary trial, it set speed limits of 60 miles per hour during the day and 50 miles per hour at night in preparation for the Fourth of July weekend in 1955.

On July 2, 1955, patrolman Ralph F. Garthwaite, a graduate of Harlan High School and a Silver Star combat veteran in World War II, was patrolling near Woodbine on US Highway 30. While crossing a 24-foot bridge, the left front fender of his patrol car collided with another vehicle traveling in the opposite direction. Garthwaite was killed. The investigation proved that the other driver was intoxicated.

Garthwaite's patrol car wreckage is seen here. Garthwaite's badge number 218 was permanently retired and a bridge on US Highway 30 near the Boyer River was dedicated in his name. Each year, a graduate of Harlan High School receives the Garthwaite Safe Driving Award.

The patrol continued its inspection of school buses. Karl Meinhard recalled, "We'd go to the schools every fall and catch the buses as they came in." James Machholz recalled, "We'd check things like brakes and lights and tell them to repair them when we found something wrong." Here, from left to right, Sgt. Andre Carstensen, patrolman Loren Dykeman, and F.W. Bohning, from the Iowa Department of Public Instruction, use checklists to inspect the school buses.

With Iowa's significant Amish communities, plenty of horse-drawn vehicles share rural roads with motorized vehicles. Here, patrolmen Melvin Hove (right) and Charles Bendlage Jr. install reflective tape on the rears of buggies following a safety inspection.

An unidentified patrolman issues a summons to a driver. Two-lane highways were soon joined by a system of "super interstate highways" across the country. When President Eisenhower signed the Federal Highway Act into law, it influenced changes in state law enforcement and safety guidelines in every state, including Iowa.

Chief David Herrick used the new Federal Highway Act to justify a long-needed increase in patrol manpower as well as a pay raise for current patrolmen. The Iowa Legislature approved an increase of 50 men, to a total of 275, including drivers examiners. Each patrolman received a pay raise of $50 per month, along with $15 per month for each five years of experience.

For a Challenging Career

INQUIRE AT NEAREST IOWA HIGHWAY PATROL OFFICE or PATROL HEADQUARTERS

STATE OFFICE BLDG. DES MOINES, IOWA

Applications Now Being Accepted

JOIN the IOWA HIGHWAY PATROL

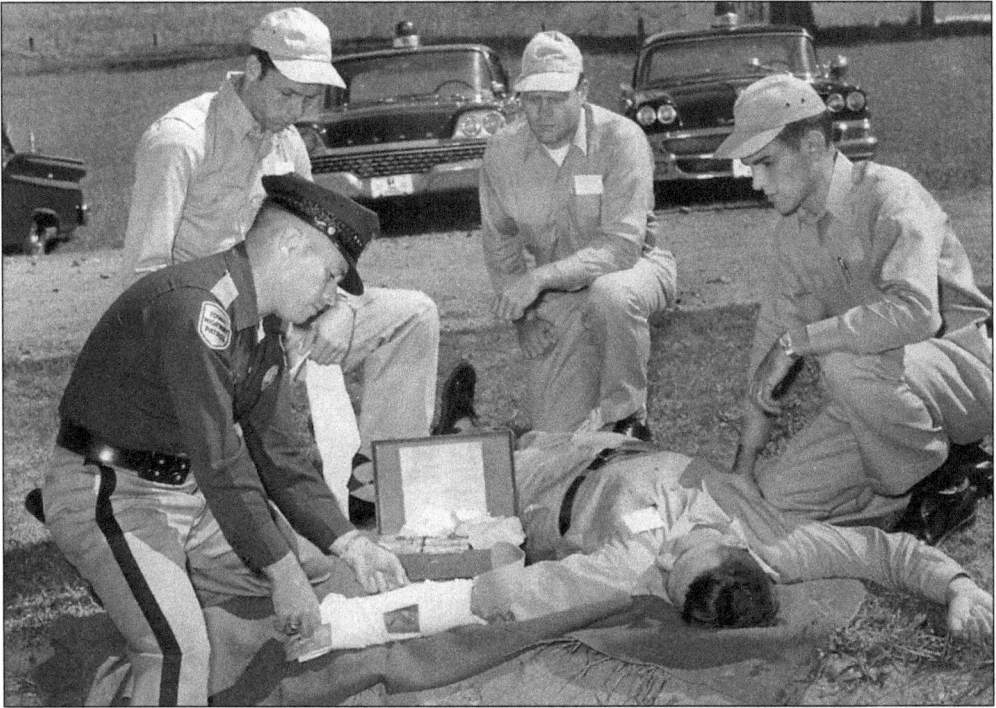

A new patrol training camp was organized by James Machholz. Many of the instructors were experienced members of the postwar training camp, like patrolman Glenn McDole, seen here demonstrating first aid to a group of recruits—from left to right, Cal Countryman, Calvin Clark, and Dick Smith, with Leland Sellers as the injured man.

In addition to the regular recruit pistol training at Camp Dodge, seen here, there was competition among Iowa law enforcement agencies for qualification to the national Colt–Indiana University pistol match at Indianapolis, as well as to the national police pistol championships, held annually in Colorado.

With established speed limits now permanently in place, new methods of monitoring vehicle speeds were tested as they were developed. Here, a "tape-type" speed meter is demonstrated at Camp Dodge. From left to right are Sgt. Cletus Stangl, Lt. Melvin Hove, technician Walt Barrett, and Capt. Don French.

The "speed tape" system, seen here, used two sensory strips placed 10 feet apart across the highway and connected to an electronic meter. The meter measured the time it took a vehicle to pass between the two strips, thus measuring the vehicle's speed. The only drawback was that a patrolman had to first disconnect the meter from his patrol car before pursuing the violating car.

David Herrick announced that for the 1955 Fourth of July weekend, the Iowa Highway Patrol and the National Guard would join in a partnership to fill Iowa's roads and skies with patrolmen and guardsman to monitor traffic. Seen here reviewing the plan are, from left to right, Capt. William Cocking of the Air National Guard and patrol officers Melvin Hove, Burnell Haven, and Harold Lorenz.

The 34th Military Police Company of the Iowa National Guard prepares to assist the Iowa Highway Patrol. Each military vehicle carries a sign that reads "Auxiliary Highway Patrol," showing drivers that anyone driving the military vehicle had enforcement authority to write speeding tickets.

87

For the holiday weekend, Iowa Highway Patrol officers monitored traffic from the skies. It began with patrolmen flying as observers with National Guard pilots, but soon evolved into patrolmen who were licensed pilots flying the aircraft. Here, patrolmen Jack Beaman goes over the flight plan with patrolman and pilot William Kemmerer at Clear Lake.

This is the patrol's first aircraft, a Piper Super Cub, which began the tradition of the air wing that continues today. The aircraft was used not only to monitor drivers on highways, but also to help locate lost children and elderly citizens and spot getaway vehicles. Two-way radios kept the aircraft in communication with patrol cars on the ground.

Patrol pistol teams consistently performed well in national shooting competitions. The 1960 team won the National Pistol Competition, held in Colorado. The champions are, from left to right, Buck Cole, Robert Glenn, Robert Lenius, Carl Lenz, Richard Ward, and Blackie Strout.

In August 1963, Ted Mikesch became chief of the patrol after the retirement of David Herrick. A native of Mason City, Mikesch had always wanted to be a patrolman as a youth and had, in fact, reached the minimum age as a recruit in the 1937 patrol training camp. During World War II, he took a leave of absence to serve in the military, returning to the patrol when the war ended.

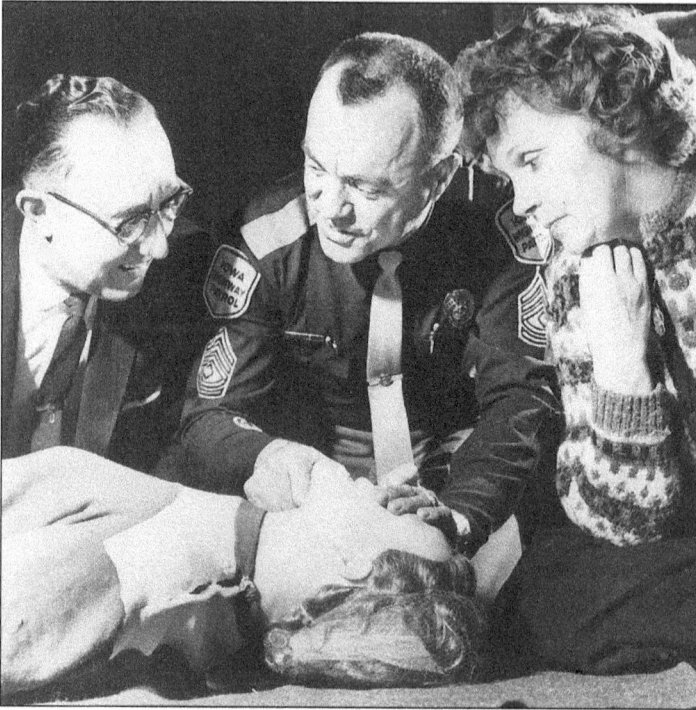

The Iowa Department of Public Instruction asked the patrol to teach short courses in first aid, initially to school bus drivers. Sgt. Robert Glenn was chosen to travel around the state to teach the seminars. The courses were so popular that Glenn's title, safety education officer, was made permanent. Here, Sgt. Glenn (center) demonstrates how to administer first aid on a "victim doll" to Rev. Clifford Gerard of Mount Ayr (left) and Ruby Bush of Lennox.

Robert Glenn did such an effective job as safety education officer that the patrol could not keep up with the demand for his training sessions. So, in 1965, five more safety education officers, supervised by Glenn, were added. Pictured, from left to right, are Glenn, Carl Lenz, Jim Bonstetter, Marvin Messerschmidt, Cal Wagner, and Bob Lutter. The men also performed regular patrolman duties in addition to their safety training assignments.

In the mid-1960s, the commissioner's office announced changes that would affect patrolmen in the field. First was the abolishment of the old points system relating to moving violations and revocation of driver's licenses, which was cited as "too cumbersome to enforce." In addition, patrolmen were ordered to enforce Iowa's Implied Consent Law, which stipulated that by signing his or her driver's license, any motorist could have it revoked by refusing to submit to the withdrawal of blood, breath, saliva, or urine in order to determine alcohol content. Also, as seen on this patrol car, radar began regular use for speed limit enforcement.

On June 11, 1965, Sgt. Marvin C. VanderLinden, a Murray, Iowa, native and a 23-year veteran of the patrol, was killed while responding to an accident call north of Sheldahl. His patrol car was struck broadside while passing through an intersection near Alleman. The impact threw both cars into the ditch, killing both drivers instantly. His badge number 46 was retired permanently and he was awarded the Medal of Valor posthumously by the National Police Officers Association. In addition, a bridge on Interstate 80 over the Des Moines River was dedicated in his name.

On Friday afternoon, October 14, 1966, a tornado slammed into the heart of Belmond, Iowa. Patrolman Bill James, driving his patrol car just ahead of the storm, warned as many citizens as he could. He rode out the storm in his car, knowing he would be needed when it was over. "I advised everyone to stay where they were. Within an hour there were about twenty-five patrolmen in the area and another fifty en route." Six people were killed, more than 250 homes were destroyed or damaged, and 75 business buildings were destroyed or badly damaged.

Bennett, Iowa, native Howard Miller became chief of the patrol in 1967. The former University of Iowa baseball player joined the patrol in 1942, left to serve in the military during World War II, and then returned to the patrol. He had served in Mason City and Iowa City and been in charge of the driver's license division.

In 1968, Maj. James Machholz designed and supervised construction of the patrol's Mobile Command Communications Center, seen here. This unit was linked to the National Crime Information Center's computer, and could be driven to any emergency location to aid officers and disaster officials. It was used on May 15 of that year, when a series of tornados ripped through northern Iowa. In all, 13 people were killed in Charles City and four died in Oelwein. Many more were injured in Elma, Maynard, and Niles Corners during one of the worst single days of storm destruction in Iowa history.

In 1970, the patrol was given the responsibility of ensuring the safety of the governor and the first family. Governor's detail responsibilities include all driving of the governor's car, setting up of all travel arrangements, and investigation of any threats against the governor or the governor's family. Here, Lt. Earl Usher, one of the first members of the governor's detail, drives Gov. Robert Ray.

By 1970, the patrol's cars changed to white. Here, Sgt. Gary Herrick, the son of former chief David Herrick, paints aircraft spotting strips on the highway in front of his new white patrol car. The white strips, set a certain distance apart, allowed an aircraft spotter, using a stopwatch, to calculate the speed of a vehicle by timing how long it took to drive between the two strips.

Members of the patrol received specialized training in controlling crowds, using riot gear in the event of prison uprisings, union picket-line clashes, and college campus demonstrations. Campus unrest and demonstrations protesting America's involvement in Southeast Asia were getting larger and more violent. Peaceful gatherings turned into window smashing and arson on the University of Iowa campus. The patrol was called in to support the Iowa City Police Department and the Johnson County Sheriff's Department.

Capt. Lyle Dickinson commanded all units, telling the protesters, "It is not my purpose to argue the rights or wrongs of any political question, but simply tell you that you are in violation of the law. We will arrest you. If you sit down, we will carry you—the decision is yours." Governor Ray commended the patrol for its professionalism. The University of Iowa's *Daily Iowan* reported, "It was simply tremendous to see the Highway Patrol relieve the city police in this tense situation. [The next day] it was commonplace to see a pair of uniformed patrolmen simply rapping with students on the Pentacrest."

GALENA

JULY 31 - AUG. 2
- NEAR WADENA, IOWA -
(MUSIC STARTS AT NOON FRI.)

SORRY FOR THE DELAY IN ANNOUNCING OUR EXACT SITE - SOME FINE CITIZENS STILL DON'T BELIEVE THAT OUR CULTURE CAN GET IT TOGETHER FOR A FEW DAYS IN AN AIR OF PEACE AND MUTUAL RESPONSIBILITY.

WE'VE TRIED VERY HARD TO RID OUR-SELVES OF THE SHORTCOMINGS OF PREVIOUS MUSIC FESTIVALS IN THE MIDWEST: EVERY BAND SCHEDULED BELOW HAS BEEN PAID IN ADVANCE - HENCE NO LAST MINUTE CAN-CELLATIONS. GEOFF COOK'S SOUND SYSTEM AND JERRY ABRAMS HEAD LIGHTS FROM SAN FRANCISCO ARE RELIABLE AND UNEXCELLED IN QUALITY. ALL CONCESSIONS ARE GUARANTEED TO BE FAIR, AND WILL IN-CLUDE A GENERAL STORE SET-UP. PROVISIONS HAVE ALSO BEEN MADE FOR MORE-THAN-ADEQUATE DRINKING WATER RESERVES AND SANITATION SERVICES TO BE ON THE SITE AT ALL TIMES.

SOME BEAUTIFUL FARMLAND WITH A CLEAN RIVER, AND SOME FINE MUSICIANS TO SET THE TONE. GALENA....NOT A HYPE, JUST A SETTING FOR AN ATMOSPHERE OF COMM-UNITY AND GOOD MUSIC. HOPE TO SEE YOU THERE -

PEACE,
SOUND STORM

TAKE U.S. 20 WEST FROM DUBUQUE
WATCH FOR "GALENA" SIGNS

$10 ADVANCE SALE, OR $15 AT THE SITE

FRIDAY		SATURDAY		SUNDAY	
SRC	ROTARY CONNECTION	JOE KELLY	FLYING BURRITO BROS.	BLOOMSBURY PEOPLE	OZ
FUSE	LEON RUSSEL	CHICKEN SHACK	ROTARY CONNECTION	WHITE LIGHTENING	GYPSY
TIM HARDIN	ILLINOIS SPEEDPRESS	MASON PROFFIT	SAVOY BROWN	IAN AND SYLVIA	GUESS WHO
MASON PROFFIT	LITTLE RICHARD	LEE MICHAELS	ALBERT KING	JOE KELLY	TERRY REID
JOHNNY WINTER	SIEGLE & SCHWALL	YOUNGBLOODS	BUFFY STE.MARIE	EVERLY BROS.	POCO
		CHAMBERS BROS.		LUTHER ALLISON	

In the summer of 1970, the patrol found itself in the middle of another controversial issue involving young people. This time, the event was an outdoor, "Woodstock-style" music festival. A Chicago-based investment company purchased 200 acres in northeast Iowa near the small town of Wadena. Promoters sent out advertisements like this one and expected the event to draw "tens of thousands of people."

Before the Wadena event started, state officials, including patrol chief Howard Miller, and representatives from the festival got together and formed a plan that provided the least amount of disruption to local citizens. The patrol's mobile command post was brought in along with 200 patrolmen, who slept on cots at the Wadena High School gymnasium. They set up roadblocks on roads leading to the festival, only letting in vehicles carrying food and festival workers. Here, patrolman Jerry Baker inspects the contents of a van.

Capt. L.E. Schellhase and Capt. Lyle Dickinson were in charge. Schellhase recalled, "I told the cook to get the best food available and make plenty of it." Lt. Vern Foughty recalled, "I remember it was hot! But the food was excellent and available twenty-four hours a day. The only incident I recall was one young lady who was running through the fields wearing only a short T-shirt. We apprehended her and escorted her to medical personnel." Governor Ray attended and addressed the crowd at the opening ceremony. No major problems were reported.

Six

INTO THE MODERN ERA

The 1970s marked the beginning of a new era for the patrol. James Machholz, the last active member of the "First Fifty" class of 1935, retired after almost 40 years of service. It also marked a new tradition, which became one of the distinctive features of every current patrol uniform, along with the brown shirts. Campaign, or flat-brim-style, hats were adopted, along with a new, round hat badge, as seen here.

The replacement of the "garrison" cap, affectionately known as the "bus driver's cap," worn by patrolman Roy Vogel (left) with the campaign hat worn by Lt. Ed Dickinson (right) was the first major change in the patrol uniform since the 1930s, when Oxford shoes replaced knee-high boots.

Gov. Robert Ray is presented with the official "first patrol campaign hat" at an office ceremony. Pictured are, from left to right, Maj. Jack Beaman; Sgt. Earl Usher, who later became chief; Sgt. Wayne Petersen; Michael Sellers, the commissioner of public safety; Governor Ray; Maj. James Machholz; and patrol chief Howard Miller.

Trooper Richard Fellin investigates an accident involving a bicycle. Through the continued efforts of Robert Glenn and the safety education officers' unit, the Schwinn Bicycle Company donated enough 10-speed bicycles to the patrol to equip each safety officer with a bicycle for the seminars they held throughout the state.

The safety education program was so successful that the patrol assigned one safety education officer to each district headquarters. The safety education officers pictured are, from left to right, (first row) Lt. Robert Glenn and troopers Cal Wagner, Carl Condon, Garland Morse, John Graham, Richard Weidman, and Dale Hanson; (second row) troopers James Bonnstetter, Larry Hutchinson, Wayne Hampton, Walter Gillette, Gene Koble, Roy Eubanks, Maynard Holland, and John Alles.

Edward Dickinson, a native of Nevada, Iowa, became the new patrol chief in 1974. He was the brother of Capt. Lyle Dickinson. Edward was a Marine Corps veteran who served in the Pacific during World War II. He had been captain in charge of the patrol's planning and operations division.

Trooper Robert Battani uses a tuning fork to calibrate the new generation of Doppler radar for his patrol car. New surveillance and communications equipment added to the effectiveness of each patrol car.

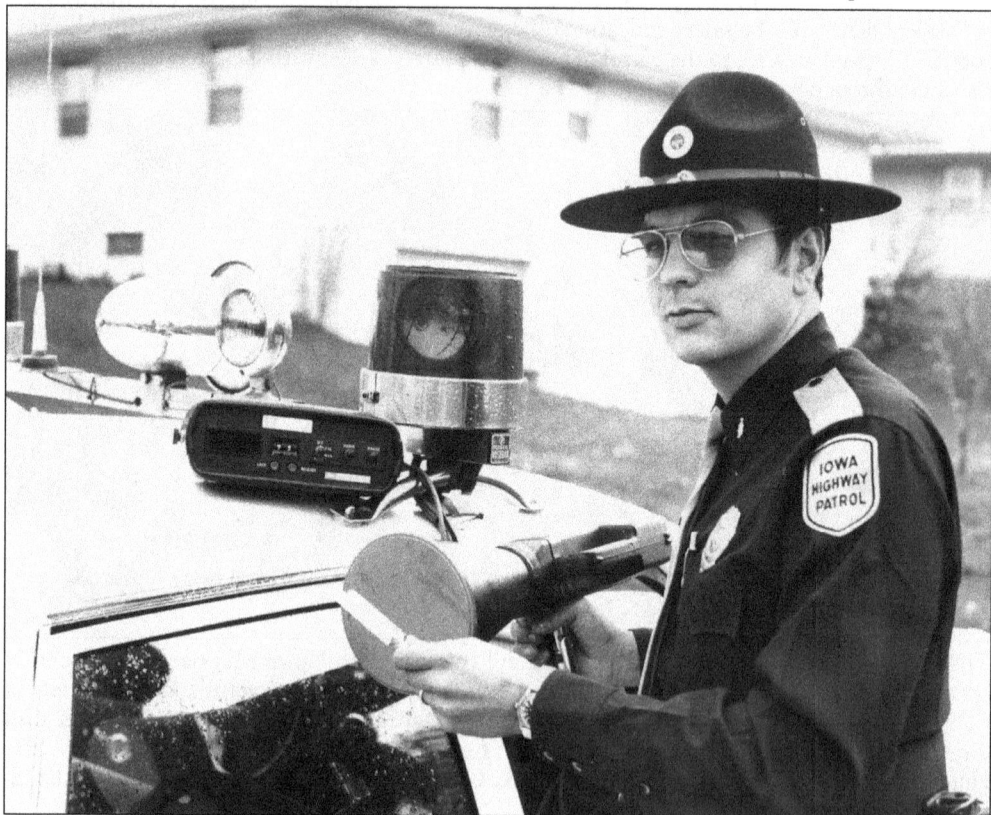

Along with the new campaign hats and hat badges, this new patrol breast badge became part of the uniform. Patrolmen were now officially known as troopers.

On July 28, 1975, on the 40th anniversary of the first Iowa Highway Safety Patrol, came a new name for the patrol itself. The former Iowa Highway Patrol was now known as the Iowa State Patrol. The new uniform shoulder patch and patrol car shield retained the same basic shape and color scheme as the previous patches. Also in 1975, the responsibility for administering driver's licenses was transferred to the Iowa Department of Transportation, where civilians took over those duties after 36 years of patrol oversight.

There were some new faces in the training academy class of 1975. One of them was Robert Thomas (far left), the first African American member of the patrol. An Army veteran, Thomas grew up in the South and graduated with a degree in agronomy from North Carolina A&T State University. He recalled, "They asked me a lot of questions about how I would handle racial slurs and things like that. It was tough, but Major Frank Metzger kept me going. He reminded me that 'once you're sworn in, you'll be sworn at for the rest of your life.'"

Following his training, Thomas became trooper number 350 and joined patrol post 12 in Davenport. "I was told that, as a rookie, you don't know anything for about five years, according to tradition," he remembers. He felt accepted once he got his first big arrest, a single-handed apprehension of a burglar at a Pleasant Valley bait shop. "One of the old timers told me that it was good police work—really dumb—but good police work. Up until then, I felt like Jackie Robinson."

Trooper Robert Thomas received the Governor's Medal of Valor, the first trooper to receive the honor, for his bravery during an extensive undercover operation in Des Moines, along with federal Bureau of Alcohol, Tobacco and Firearms agent Alex Parker.

Trooper Thomas also became an instructor at the Iowa Law Enforcement Academy, preparing other young recruits for their service on the patrol or with the Iowa Bureau of Criminal Investigation.

In 1975, Mason City native Joe Diaz was hired, making him the first Hispanic trooper. He later became an agent with the Iowa Bureau of Criminal Investigation. Later that year, the first female candidates were accepted to the Iowa Law Enforcement Training Academy. They are, from left to right, Julie Gay of Ottumwa, Gayle Adrian of Davenport, and Jen Saunders of Sioux City. Gay recalled, "I could see the looks on some of the others' faces that said, 'What's *she* doing here?'" Gay and Adrian successfully completed their training and were assigned to Winterset and Des Moines, respectively.

Capt. Donna Bacus started on the patrol in 1977 and later became the first female promoted to patrol sergeant, then lieutenant, and then captain. She recalled, "I was fortunate that other women had gone before me as Patrol officers. By the time I made sergeant, I wasn't much of a rarity because I'd been around so long and they knew me. I am more proud to wear this uniform than anything I've done." Some women were from a law enforcement family. "My father and brothers were Des Moines City law enforcement officers," explained Sgt. Barbara Malone. In 2010, trooper Yvonne Ohlensehlen became the first female trooper to retire from the patrol.

In this photograph, trooper and safety education officer Mary Skaggs teaches a D.A.R.E. class to elementary school children. Sgt. Regina Clemens, the supervisor of safety education officers, described her experience at the training academy: "The first time I shot a gun was at the Academy. My hand would actually bleed as I tried to hold the gun and it would kick." Trooper Sharon Kurt explained, "We'd get up at 'oh-dark-thirty' and run for half an hour and then go to breakfast, but once you made it through the Academy, you were accepted."

Trooper Brenda Rinard described being accepted as an equal: "If I'm sitting at a table full of troopers and someone comes over to ask a question, they always ask one of the guys. That's okay—I let them take it. You have to have a lot of humor on this job—you can't be a prude." Trooper and safety education officer Pam Brockman added, "As women, we don't have that 'macho thing' to prove like the guys do." This photograph shows three modern-day troopers of the Iowa State Patrol on duty. From left to right, they are Beth Rouse, number 223; John Simmons, number 274; and Glen Swanson, number 439. (Courtesy of ISP major Timothy Leinen, number 222; and Sgt. Thomas Lampe, number 208.)

THE IOWA POLL—Institutional Confidence

How Iowans rate their confidence in 39 governmental, business, religious and social institutions. Confidence rating number is based on a scale of one (lowest confidence) through six (highest).

	Rating Number	Rated Favorably (4-5-6)	Rated Unfavorably (1-2-3)	Don't Know
1. God	5.34	91%	7%	2%
2. State Highway Patrol	4.48	84	12	4
3. Banks and financial institutions	4.35	81	17	2
4. Medical profession	4.32	78	21	1
5. Hospitals	4.22	77	22	1
6. Organized religion and churches	4.18	71	25	4
7. Local school system	3.98	72	24	4
8. President of the United States	3.96	67	31	2
9. Local law enforcement	3.96	68	30	2
10. Universities and colleges	3.95	70	24	6
11. Local telephone company	3.93	65	32	3
12. Grocery and food stores	3.89	68	30	2
13. Des Moines Register and Tribune	3.73	67	23	10
14. U.S. Armed Forces	3.71	61	32	7
15. Major department stores	3.69	63	32	5
16. News media	3.68	59	39	2
17. The FBI	3.63	59	33	8
18. Local Chamber of Commerce	3.62	62	29	9
19. Architects, engineers and builders	3.57	60	31	9
20. Consumer protection groups	3.57	59	34	7
21. Legal profession	3.56	59	36	5
22. Local government—city and county	3.55	57	40	3
23. Judges and the courts	3.44	56	40	4
24. Insurance companies	3.41	53	43	4
25. Environmental protection groups	3.33	54	37	9
26. Gas and electric companies	3.29	50	48	2
27. United Nations	3.19	51	39	10
28. U.S. Postal Service	3.18	44	54	2
29. State Legislature	3.18	47	45	8
30. Big industrial manufacturers	3.17	46	46	8
31. Computers	3.16	46	45	9
32. Congress	3.06	43	51	6
33. U.S. Department of Agriculture	3.02	44	46	10
34. Real estate agents	2.93	38	54	7
35. Iowa Farm Bureau	2.86	48	28	24
36. State government regulatory agencies	2.82	38	51	11
37. Federal government regulatory agencies	2.76	33	58	9
38. Organized labor	2.72	33	61	6
39. Farm organizations (except Farm Bureau)	2.45	36	36	28

In 1977, patrol headquarters was moved to the Henry A. Wallace State Office Building on the state capitol complex, a uniquely designed structure with mirrored windows. It was also the first year that troopers were issued bulletproof vests, and it marked the beginning of the patrol emergency response team. Trooper Fred Herman, a member of that team, was shot in the head during a standoff at a home in Sabula. He recalled, "The shot traveled about sixty-five feet and struck me in the right temple entering my skull. I spent twelve days at Dubuque Mercy Hospital." Trooper Herman made a complete recovery and returned to duty with the .22 slug still in his head.

In 1978, the *Des Moines Register* conducted a poll of adult readers asking them to rate their level of confidence among 39 government, business, religious, and social institutions. When the votes were counted, God placed first, with a 91 percent favorability rating. In second place was the Iowa State Patrol, with an 84 percent favorability rating.

In October 1979, Pope John Paul II arrived in Iowa to visit the Living History Farms at West Des Moines. More than 300,000 people were expected to attend the event. It took weeks of preparation to ensure that all traffic and security issues were met for the visit to go smoothly. Maj. Loren Dykeman, of the patrol's logistics team, recalled, "Not only was the mix-master area a shuttle route, but we also turned it into a giant parking lot for the hundreds of buses." The event went smoothly as planned.

Motorcycles had not been used regularly since World War II, but in 1979, the patrol purchased two Kawasaki motorcycles for road patrol during summer months. Seen here from left to right are troopers Steven Heckenbach, Joseph Meola, Michael Gilbert, Robert Alles, and Gary Hoskin.

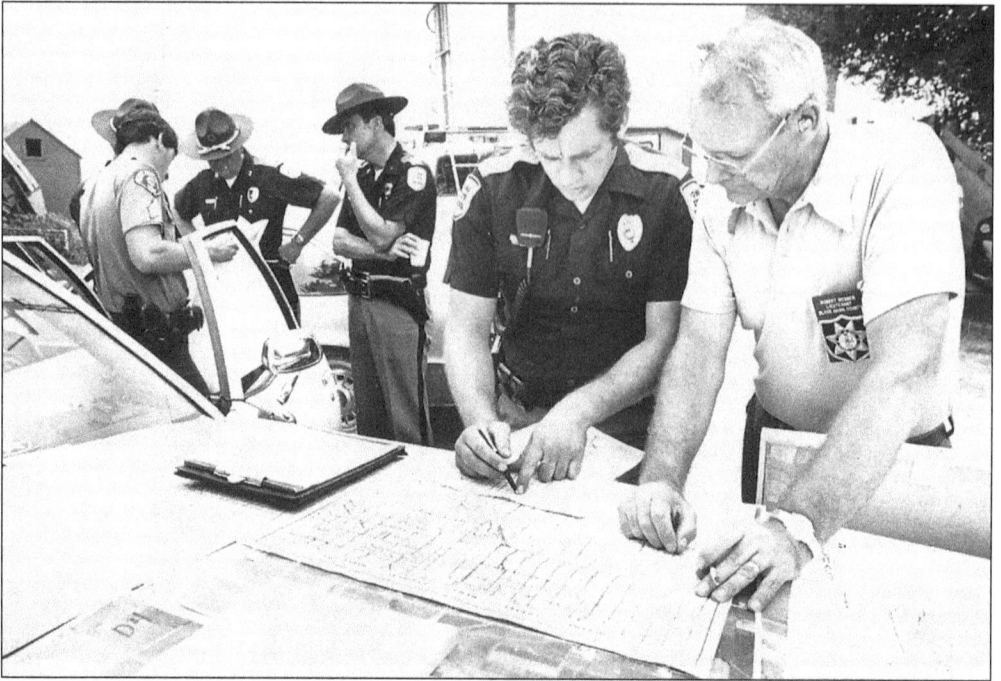

On July 13, 1981, two Waterloo police officers, Tom Rice and Michael Hoing, were gunned down by James Michael "T-Bone" Taylor as they responded to a complaint of loud music. An all-out search involving local, county, state, and federal law enforcement agencies was quickly organized. Above, trooper Michael Gilbert (left), of the Iowa State Patrol, and Black Hawk County sheriff Lt. Bob Webber look over county maps at the search command center.

During the search, a sheriff's patrol car collided with another vehicle, killing county deputy Sgt. William Milliken. Patrol trooper Marvin Messerschmidt and six Waterloo police officers began a foot search aided by patrol and National Guard aircraft flying over the tall cornfields near LaPorte City. Messerschmidt recalled, "I saw something moving and figured it might be him. I told him not to move and had my shotgun pointed right at him. It all happened so fast I didn't have time to think." Here, Trooper Messerschmidt (far right) follows Taylor, who is flanked by Waterloo officers Tom Shimp (left) and Larry Coffin.

In September 1981, inmates at Fort Madison Penitentiary rioted. A prisoner was stabbed to death, and 12 hostages were taken, including the chief security officer and eight guard trainees. Several fires were also set. The governor's office called in the Iowa State Patrol to take charge of the situation. Capt. Lyle Dickinson recalled, "They wanted us to give up our weapons before we went in." This squad of troopers arrives at the prison.

It was finally decided that the patrol's relatively new tactical team would lead the way, with the rest of the patrol members in support. Capt. Lyle Dickinson recalled, "We used four-man teams with side arms and sergeants with shotguns. It was something to see. They took over right now and no prisoner could say he had been hurt or abused. It was pure professionalism." Here, "TAC" team members, from left to right, Donald Niederhauser, Maurice Parker, and Sgt. John Quinn deploy from a helicopter at the prison.

In October 1982, Frank Metzger succeeded Edward Dickinson as patrol chief. Metzger was a graduate of Drake University and a Marine Corps veteran. He joined the patrol in 1951 and was the first training officer in 1968. His two sons, Michael and Frank Jr., were also patrol officers.

The patrol honor guard was formed in 1982 on a volunteer basis. Here, honor guard members participate in the funeral of the patrol's first chief, John Hattery.

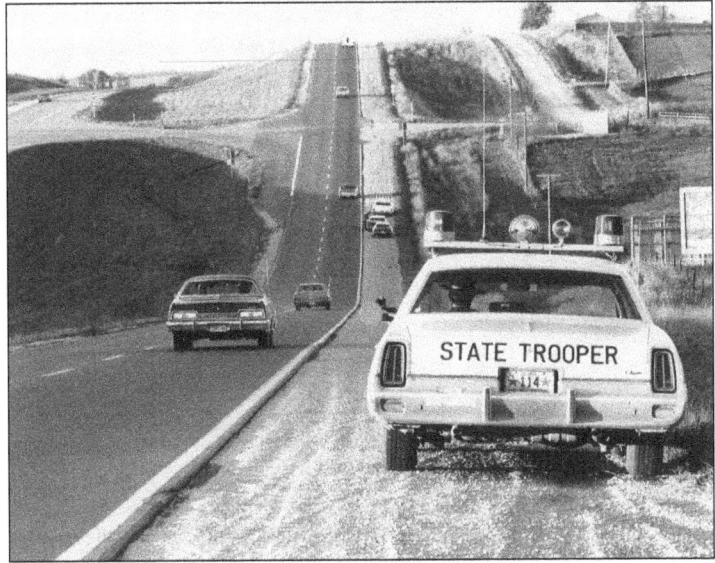

Patrol cars began the switch from white to beige in 1983. Troopers were issued Smith & Wesson Model 686 .357 Magnum service revolvers. It was also the beginning of the use of PR-24 batons. Here, trooper Robert Battani's Chrysler patrol car using Doppler radar partners with trooper Rex Phares farther on. Note the brake lights of the car that has just passed Battani's patrol car. (Courtesy of Robert Battani.)

Trooper and pilot Keith Millard was flying over Interstate 80 in his Patrol Cessna 172 one day in 1984. Upon his return to the Cedar Rapids Airport, he discovered that his aircraft had been hit by a .30 caliber slug, which had entered the underside of the aircraft's right wing, nicking the wing rib and just missing the fuel tank. Millard said, "If it would have hit the gas tank, the plane would have gone up like a torch." Here, fellow trooper and pilot Jerry Law (left) stands with Millard in front of a patrol Cessna 172.

On Sunday afternoon, June 16, 1985, during the patrol's 50th anniversary year, trooper Charles G. Whitney was stopping speeders on Interstate 380 near Evansville. While Whitney was handing a ticket to a driver, another vehicle, whose driver had apparently fallen asleep at the wheel, struck the officer, killing him instantly. The 54-year-old Whitney was one month away from retirement from the patrol. His badge number 329 was permanently retired and a bridge that traverses the Cedar River at Interstate 380 and US Highway 20 was dedicated in his name.

In 1988, Blaine Goff became the new patrol chief. The Washington, Iowa, native and Marine Corps veteran joined the patrol in 1956. A relative of Ola Babcock Miller, Goff was assigned to posts in Waukon, Mount Vernon, and Iowa City before becoming sergeant and assistant district commander in Davenport. He was later promoted to lieutenant and district commander in Cedar Falls. In 1983, he was promoted to captain and assigned to Des Moines headquarters as executive assistant to the commissioner.

In July 1988, the patrol assigned 22 troopers to the vehicle identification officer program to comply with the newly passed law requiring detailed inspections on salvage vehicles. Officers now conduct detailed inspections of all component parts, verifying that the vehicle or parts are not stolen. They also assist the patrol vehicle theft unit. Here, trooper Keith Wilcox inspects for a hidden confidential number.

The patrol vehicle theft unit was officially formed in 1976 as a direct result of the attempted assassination of patrol sergeant Wilton Lewis, who helped break up a vehicle theft ring in Mount Pleasant. Lt. Loren Dykeman was named as the unit coordinator and was sent to FBI training. In all, 14 troopers were assigned part-time duty as vehicle identification officers, in addition to their regular duties. Roadblocks like the one here are occasionally set up to check for stolen vehicles.

The Gold Star Museum, near Des Moines at Camp Dodge, includes an Iowa State Patrol exhibit displaying artifacts such as uniforms, license plates, photographs, and other memorabilia related to the history of the Iowa State Patrol. Chief Goff assigned trooper Michael Horihan as curator. Capt. Shane Antle and Sgt. Regina Clemens coordinated the establishment of the display in the museum building.

The annual Iowa State Fair is one of the largest and most-attended state fairs in the country. The Iowa State Patrol has always been a visible presence at the event going back to the patrol's founding in 1935. Here, troopers Dennis Hawkins (left) and John Gilbert visit with young fairgoers from their patrol cart.

On June 30, 1989, the Cass County Sheriff's Department contacted the patrol for help in searching for an elderly man who had wandered away from his nursing home. Trooper and pilot Lance G. Dietsch (right) was piloting the patrol's Maule aircraft as trooper Stanley Gerling (below) was acting as spotter. About 5:45 p.m., just as the sun was setting, the men spotted the man in a field and began circling at an altitude of about 200 feet, leading the search team on the ground to the man's location.

Without any warning, the nose of the Maule dipped sharply and the aircraft crashed into the ground. One of the men was killed instantly, while the other died at Cass County Memorial Hospital shortly thereafter. They were the first troopers killed in a patrol aircraft since the establishment of the patrol air wing in 1957. Dietsch's badge number 142 and Gerling's badge number 190 were permanently retired and a bridge on US Highway 6 west of Lewis at Indian Creek was dedicated in the fallen troopers' names.

115

A little more than a year after the deaths of Dietsch and Gerling, there was another tragic accident involving the patrol's air wing. On October 14, 1990, trooper and pilot Allen Nieland took off in his patrol Cessna 172 to help in the pursuit of a robbery suspect driving a stolen pickup truck south of Little Amana. Nieland spotted the suspect vehicle traveling near US Highway 151 and began circling as the troopers on the ground converged on the area. Suddenly, the aircraft nose-dived into the ground in a field next to a motel.

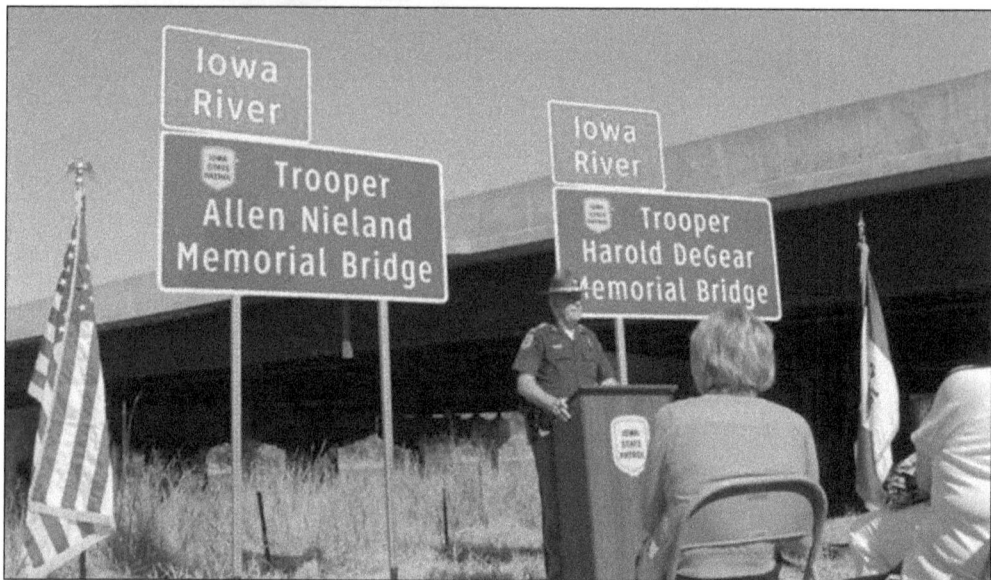

The severity of the impact and resulting explosion killed Nieland instantly, even though rescuers were on the scene immediately and tried to put out the fire. The suspect was later apprehended and charged with vehicular homicide. Nieland left a wife and four children. His badge number 445 was permanently retired. This bridge, on westbound Interstate 80 and northbound Interstate 380 traversing the Iowa River, also named for patrolman Harold DeGear, was dedicated for Nieland.

In 1992, upon patrol chief Blaine Goff's retirement, Earl Usher became the new chief of the Iowa State Patrol. The 31-year veteran of the patrol and native of Nashua, Iowa, was first assigned to Indianola in 1961 before being selected for the governor's detail in 1970. In 1976, Usher became head of the capitol police division and coordinated the patrol's community service program. He said, "I just want to make sure the image of the State Patrol remains as it is today. We need to be ready to move forward." He promoted new initiatives such as the installation of camcorders in patrol cars and oversaw the implementation of the Motor Carrier Safety Assistance and Motorist Assistance Programs.

The patrol canine unit also began in 1992. The original five canines and their trooper partners are seen here. Pictured are, from left to right, Eldean Maketzke and Gus; Don McGlaughlin and Bullet; Col. Earl Usher; Bill Hon and Taz; Tom Estrada and Charley; Phil Perkins and Jager; and Lt. Gary Herrick. Trooper Tom Estrada said, "You have to believe in the dog and support him a hundred percent."

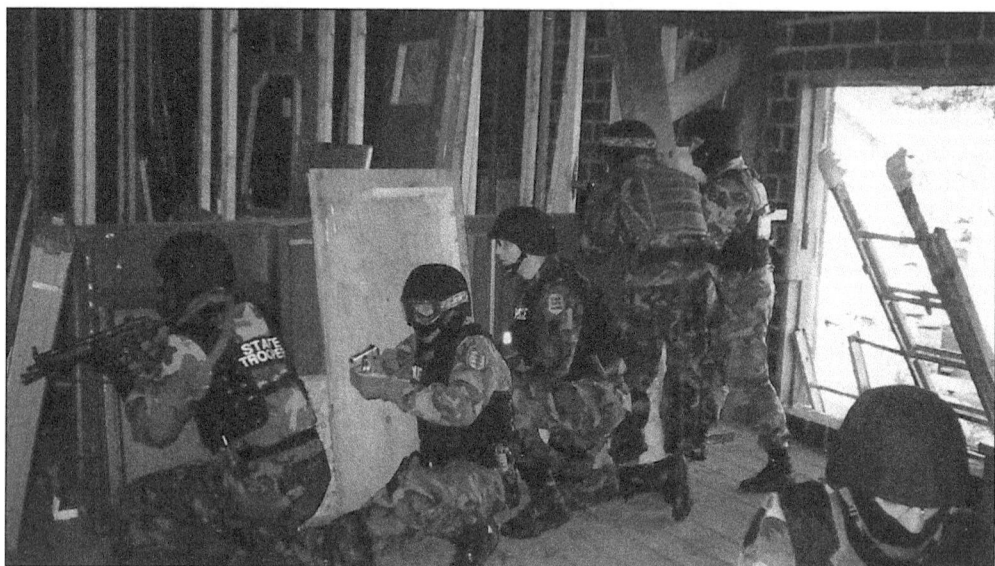

Tactical teams continued their cutting-edge training with an emphasis on drug raids and prison riots. The primary mission of the tactical teams is to provide a specially-equipped, highly-trained unit.

Additional pistol range training was required for all members when the patrol adopted the Smith & Wesson Model 4046 .40 caliber semiautomatic as the official sidearm.

During the great floods of 1993, troopers were deployed to assist cities and counties with traffic control and other flood-related duties. Portions of many main highways, and even interstates, had to be closed, some of them for weeks at a time.

Monroe native and 30-year patrol veteran Jon Wilson became the new patrol chief in July 1996 after the retirement of Earl Usher. One of Wilson's first duties was to coordinate training programs for the patrol's new firearms training simulator, or FATS. This $110,000 unit, using computer software like a very realistic video arcade game, created various scenarios during which troopers could test their reaction skills in situations where they would have to make a split-second decision whether to shoot or not to shoot.

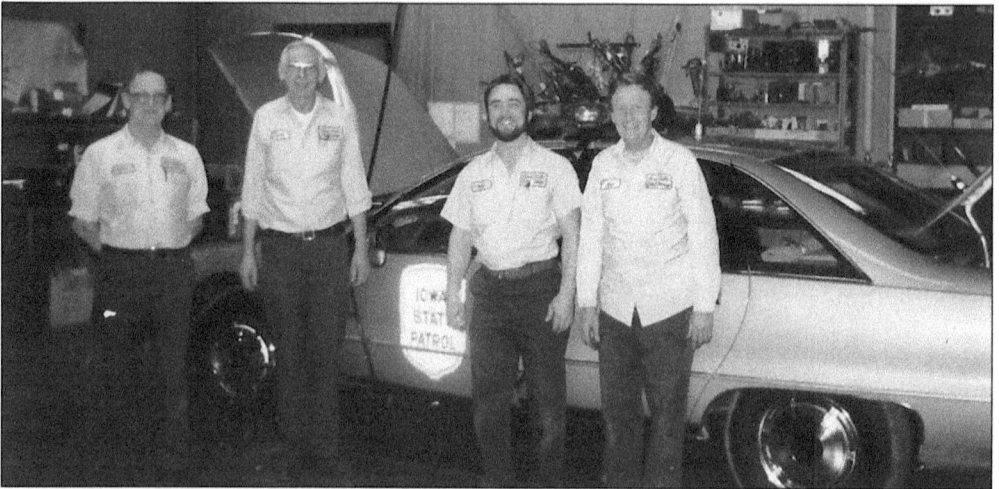

The Iowa State Patrol has its own vehicle maintenance garage in Des Moines. From left to right, John McGinnes, Carl Stoecker, Michael Brinks, and Al Hokanson prepare the cars for road duty. John Tate was also a member of the vehicle maintenance staff.

Part of Iowa's summer tradition is the "coast-to-coast" Register's Annual Great Bicycle Ride Across Iowa, or RAGBRAI. Each year, a new route from the Missouri River to the Mississippi River is established for the six-day event. The Iowa State Patrol helps plan the route and supports the participants, keeping them safe. Here, trooper Michael Horihan coordinates traffic with the RAGBRAI participants.

In October 1999, when Jon Wilson retired, Robert O. Garrison (shown here) became the new chief. The Emmetsburg native held bachelor's and master's degrees in nursing from Drake University. The same year, Charles "Buck" Cole, the last surviving retiree of the original "First Fifty" class, died.

By 2000, the patrol was organized into 16 districts, compared to its original four areas in 1935.

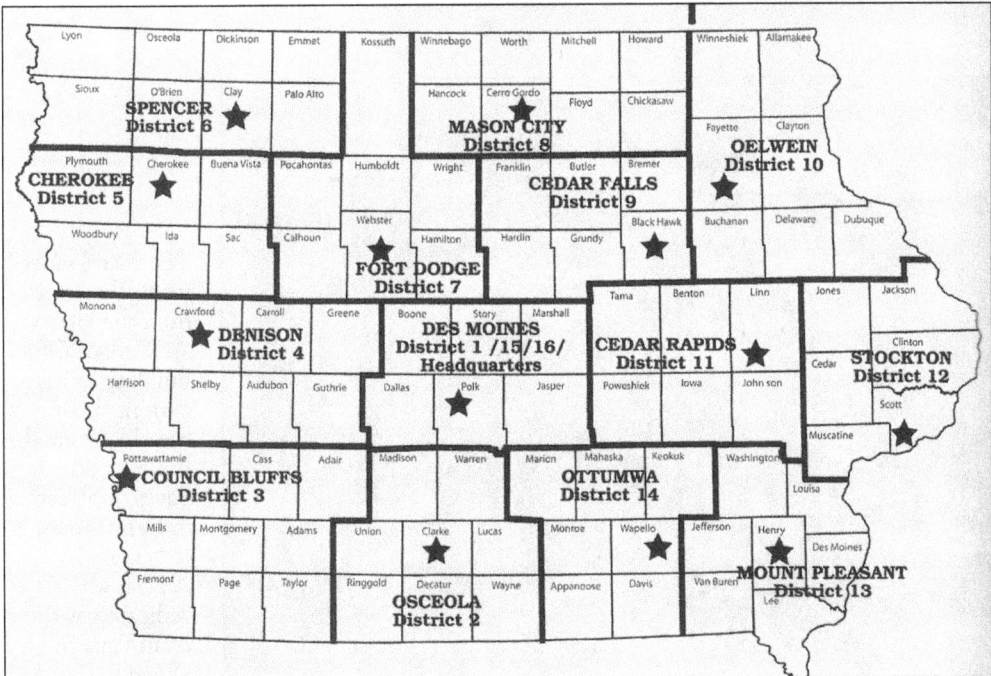

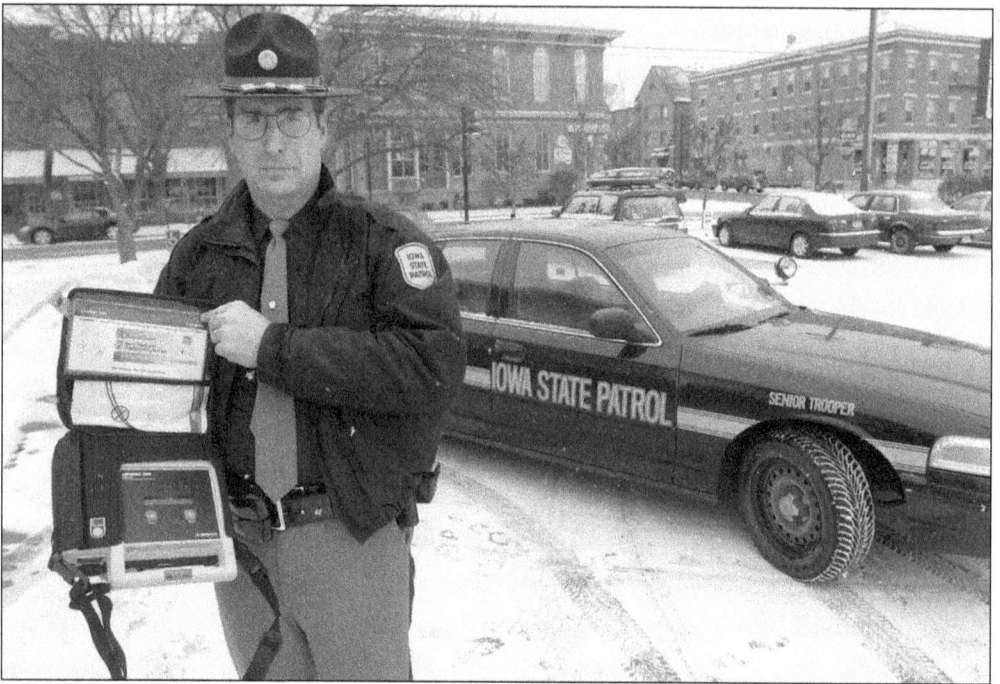

In 2003, after more than 60 years using the cross-draw holster, the patrol shifted the location of its service sidearm to the "strong side." Also in 2003, trooper Michael Horihan, seen here, became the first to have a defibrillator as standard equipment for his patrol car. It was purchased as a result of a generous gift from the Coralville North Corridor Rotary Club.

The patrol moved its headquarters from the Henry A. Wallace Office Building to its current site in the old Armand Building on Seventh Street in Des Moines, seen here. In 2012, it was dedicated as the Oran Pape State Office Building.

In 2007, Patrick J. Hoye, a Storm Lake native, became the new chief. Hoye joined in 1982, served 14 years in District 5 (Cherokee), was promoted to sergeant in Mount Pleasant, lieutenant in Spencer, then captain in Des Moines. He was Iowa's D.A.R.E. coordinator and supervised Iowa State Fair's security. He is a graduate of the FBI National Academy and Drake University's certified public management course. While he was colonel, the patrol initiated the dedication of bridges for troopers killed in the line of duty.

Also in 2007, Dodge Charger patrol cars were added to the fleet. In addition, two Cessna 182s were obtained to replace aging air wing aircraft. The installation of in-car computers to all troopers' cars was completed as well, and rifles were issued to all troopers. In 2008, the patrol was recognized by the International Association of Chiefs of Police (IACP) as the top state policing agency for its size.

In 2010, the patrol celebrated its 75th anniversary. Representing historic patrol vehicles and uniforms in a photograph organized by Lt. Gene Hill are, from left to right, troopers Robert Messelheiser, Robert Glenn, Robert Alles, and Kathleen Burdock. Chief Hoye said, "The one thing that has remained steadfast is our goal to serve."

Seen here is the early patrol car (left), which had a tube-type AM radio receiver only, and no transmitter. That was the extent of the "extra features" making it a patrol vehicle. The modern patrol car (right) is not only bigger, faster, and more reliable, it is a rolling digital communications platform, providing the trooper with instant access to databases for information as well as the ability to transmit and receive globally at any time.

124

On the afternoon of September 8, 2011, trooper Mark Toney was killed while answering a call about two miles south of Indianola. Toney's patrol car was heading north on US Highway 65/69 with its top lights on when it hit the shoulder of the road, rolled several times into a field, and caught fire. By the time rescuers arrived on the scene, the car was completely engulfed in flames. The 43-year-old Toney, a 24-year veteran of the patrol, was pronounced dead at the scene.

This photograph shows the patrol honor guard and ranks of troopers at trooper Mark Toney's funeral. His badge number 227 was permanently retired. The South River Bridge on US Highway 65/69 south of Indianola was also dedicated in his name.

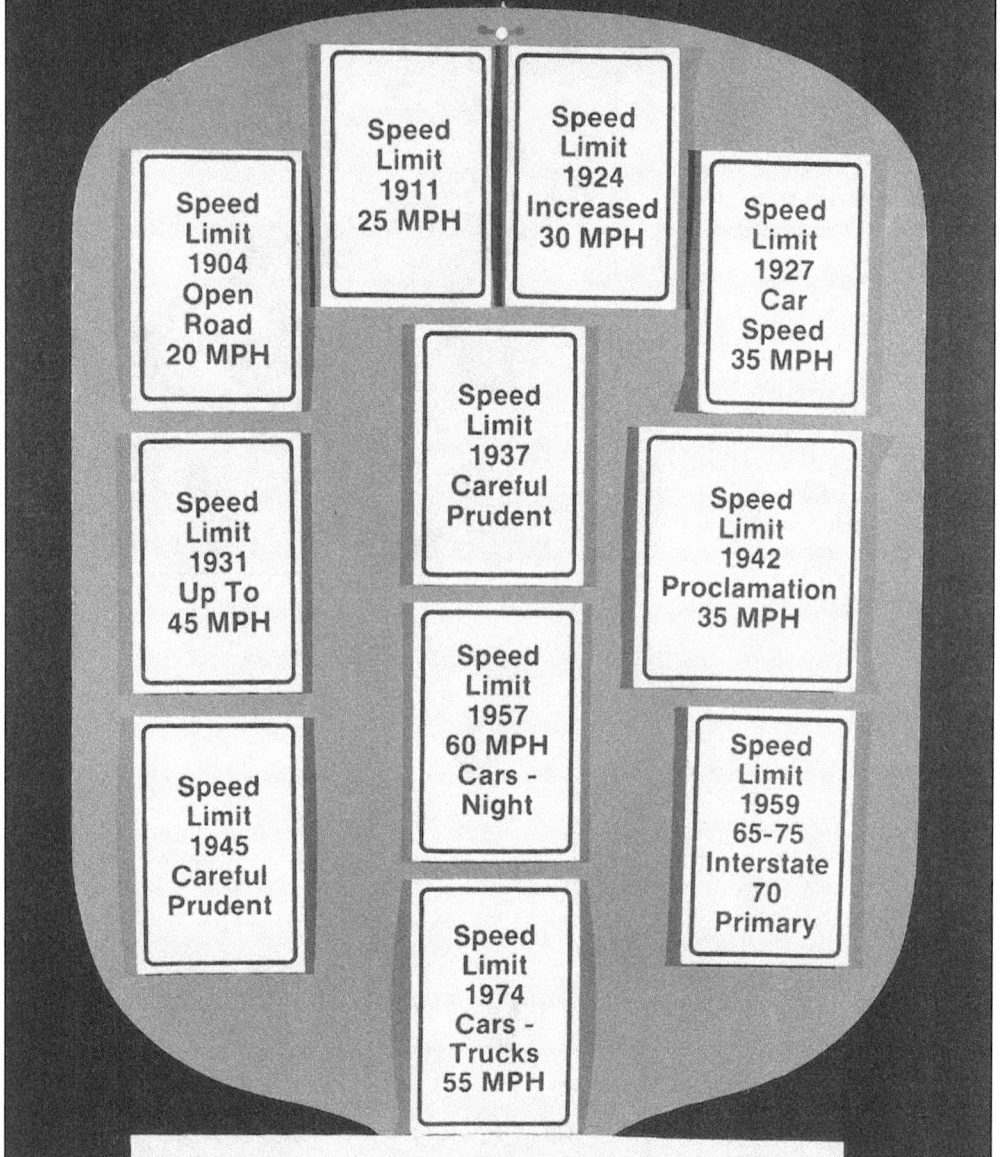

SPEED LIMITS

Speed Limit 1904 Open Road 20 MPH

Speed Limit 1911 25 MPH

Speed Limit 1924 Increased 30 MPH

Speed Limit 1927 Car Speed 35 MPH

Speed Limit 1931 Up To 45 MPH

Speed Limit 1937 Careful Prudent

Speed Limit 1942 Proclamation 35 MPH

Speed Limit 1945 Careful Prudent

Speed Limit 1957 60 MPH Cars - Night

Speed Limit 1959 65-75 Interstate 70 Primary

Speed Limit 1974 Cars - Trucks 55 MPH

This display of signs traces the evolution of the state's speed limits from 1904's "20 MPH" to 1937's "careful/prudent" to 1957's "60 MPH Cars–Night," to 1974's "Cars–Trucks 55 MPH."

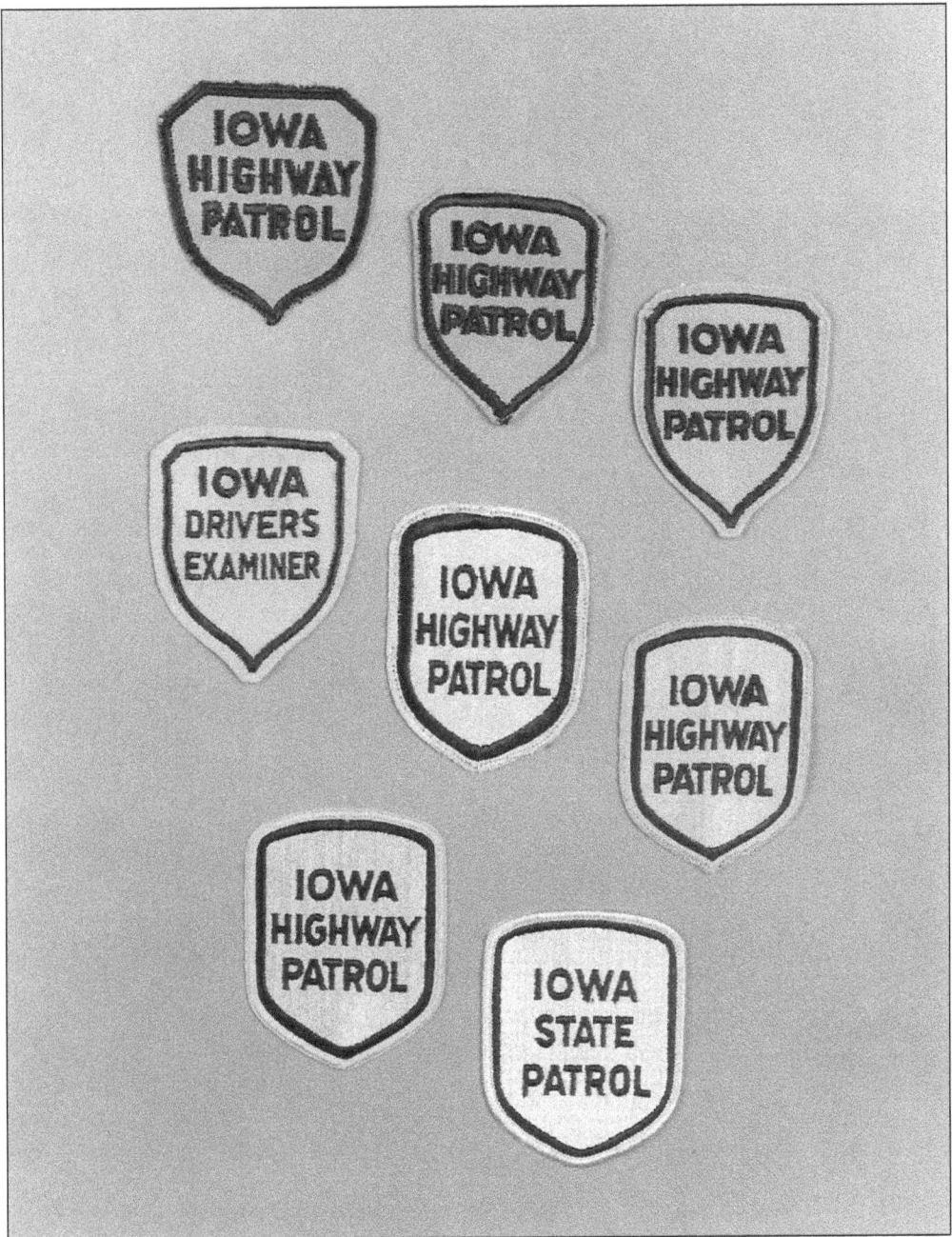

This display shows the 75-year tradition of the original Iowa Highway Patrol "corn kernel" shoulder patch and shield. Today's Iowa State Patrol patch represents the overall respect for tradition that current troopers have regarding those "First Fifty" patrolmen, while realizing the importance of moving forward with necessary changes. Even with all the new technologies, improved systems, and increases in personnel, the members of that 1935 class and Ola Babcock Miller would recognize the commitment of today's troopers to Buck Cole's patrol motto of "Courtesy-Service-Protection."

Visit us at
arcadiapublishing.com